RAM
A Global History

Ameya Pratap Singh

A Global Order presentation

RAM – A Global History
Ameya Pratap Singh

First published in 2024 by **Global Order**
an imprint of Grin Media Private Limited

Milap Niketan, 8A, Bahadur Shah Zafar Marg, New Delhi, Delhi-110002
www.globalorder.live || www.grin.news

ISBN 978-81-949701-5-6

Typeset in Adobe Caslon Pro

Printed and Bound in India by R. K. Print Solution.

To Papa,
For always finding the best in me

Acknowledgements

The idea for this book was the result of a late evening phone call with my dear friend and brother, Dr. Hindol Sengupta. We've shared lots of good food, conversations, and camaraderie over the years, and it is my great fortune to have worked with him on this project. I wouldn't accept it if he wasn't publishing the book, and I still do so begrudgingly, but he has an uncanny genius for choosing themes that demand popular attention and spur debate, and to the extent that readers of this book find its subject interesting, it is him to be credited.

As an academic and writer, I owe an extraordinary debt to my PhD supervisor, Dr. Kate Sullivan de Estrada. Not only did she show me the ropes in the academy, I also learnt empathy and humility from her. I cannot understate how much her unwavering support meant during my time as a doctoral student at the University of Oxford. I also owe thanks for past mentorship to Dr. Shailaja Fennell and Dr. Joya Chatterji from my time at the University of Cambridge, and to Dr. James Strong and Dr. Christopher Coker from my time at the London School of Economics. I shared a special bond with Chris and it's a shame he won't read the contents of this book as he had grown particularly interested in the role of culture in world politics towards his later years. I hope I've done justice to his memory.

None of my scholarship would have been possible without the love and support of my parents, and in particular my father, whose devotion to Lord Ram has been a strong inspiration for this book. I've grown up on a steady diet of Indian mythology, and despite my best intentions, it would seem that I have developed a natural affinity for the stories that define India's past and the cultural fabric of her people. Every historian must choose the stories that they believe are worth telling. And sometimes we do so because these stories are part of our constitutive nature: an expression of what we know and who we are. I am also grateful to my fiancé, Ananya, for her love and support. Despite my peculiarities, she is kind, patient, and forgiving, certainly more than I merit. As my partner, she has been a sounding board for my ideas and is fully deserving of any acclaim this book project may receive.

I am also indebted to my many friends in the academy over the years, especially those that were part of the Seminar on the History of International Politics at Oxford. They are my comrades, and all of them shared, if not exceeded, my love for historical enquiry.

Contents

Introduction

Lord Ram as a Phenom of Cultural Globalisation

With the coming of the Asian Century, the cultural moorings of the ostensible "East" have received renewed historical attention. Just as, in Francis Fukuyama's famous words, history had come to an "end"[1] of sorts with the rise of American hegemony after the Cold War, it has now "resumed" with the reappearance of multipolarity—both in a political and cultural sense. Singaporean Diplomat Kishore Mahbubani's fabled manuscript in 1998 aptly titled "Can Asians Think?"[2] and the Iranian philosopher Hamid Dabashi's 2015 masterpiece "Can Non-Europeans Think?"[3] bookmark this historical turn that has slowly unravelled over the last two decades. This book too is firmly ensconced in this tradition of revisionism. In 2024, as the Ram Mandir marks the long-awaited second coming of Lord Ram to Ayodhya and the latter's restoration as a site of Hindu pilgrimage and worship, this book will look to restore the story of Lord Ram and the foremost ancient Hindu epic of the Ramayana to the annals of Global History.

One of the major challenges of this intellectual undertaking is the popularity of the Ramayana. It is so widely spread in the social imaginary of Asia that it is difficult to offer a novel and noteworthy commentary. But the stories of its travels are lesser known. It is the purpose of this book to uncover the mysteries of the Ramayana's export outside India, in Asia and beyond. How did an ancient Hindu epic travel to and become a staple in geographies and amongst people not of its own? What does this tell us about Hindu India and its influence on the shaping of pre-modern Asia? We find local retellings of the Ramayana in countries as varied as Thailand, Myanmar, Indonesia, Cambodia, Malaysia, Philippines, Japan, Laos, Sri Lanka, China, Tibet, Nepal, Singapore, Mongolia, Vietnam, and South Korea. The text is a major thread in the culture, religion, history, literature, dance in these countries, and is evident in their extensive traditions of oral storytelling, art, and architecture. In this reading the Ramayana almost comes to represent an antecedent for Hindu India's stature as a "Vishwaguru", and a global history of ethics beyond nationalism and cultural exceptionalism. As the scholar Paula Richman has argued, "since people for whom Ramayana is central now live throughout the globe… it has indeed become a global text as well as a global piece of theatre".[4] Indisputably, the Ramayana, one of the most important literary works of ancient India, has had a profound influence on art and culture outside the Indian subcontinent, especially in Southeast Asia.

There are several interesting aspects to the Ramayana's global history. First, the type of cultural globalisation it represents is exemplary of pre-modern Asia. Andrew Phillips and Jason Sharman in their book "International Order in Diversity" found that the intensity of historical interaction between cultures in the Indian Ocean Region between 1500–1750 did not lead to hegemony or homogeneity. Counter-intuitively, it led to increased heterogeneity.

Cultural dialogue between mighty Asian empires did not threaten the erasure of their political communities. Instead, it laid the foundations for their economic and cultural enrichment despite the localisation of what could be deemed as "foreign influences".[5] This is especially striking with respect to a Hindu mythological text such as the Ramayana which is steeped in the "topography of the land of India" and espouses "a fundamentally locative or place-oriented world view".[6]

This is quite similar to the spread of the Ramayana to other parts of Asia. The Ramayana did not promote a proselytising spirit akin to that of Christian crusaders or Islamic conquerors, and neither did its ideals endanger the legitimacy of other Asian emperors and their political projects. Instead, there was an organic and local diffusion of the Ramayana's ethics and principles. If sovereignty was a concept exported by Europe and localised in the rest of the world[7], the Ramayana was an epic exported by Hindu India and localised in the rest of Asia. But crucially the latter's transmission was not shrouded in the gore of violence. By no means was Asia a region devoid of politics, war, and conflict. But its peoples still knew how to engage in cultural dialogue that was distinctly non-invasive to its recipients. Perhaps a discovery of why this was so would offer some practical solutions to the ills of the modern world.

Another puzzling feature that will be uncovered in the following chapters is why the Ramayana became such a singular success in terms of the cultural exports of Hindu India. There is of course no dearth of ancient Hindu epics. So, why did the Ramayana become so popular but not others? For instance, Ravi Dutt Bajpai has argued that the

"Ramayana achieved a more profound and much wider influence on Southeast Asian societies than the Mahabharata, transmitting Indian thoughts on the code of conduct for individuals, society, states, and the international".[8] Not only this, the Ramayana was localised and popularised to such a great extent that it survived the test of time and political making and remaking across centuries, and continues to have great cultural significance in Asian countries. This indicates that the ideals it espoused on righteousness, valour, sacrifice, etc. had, and indeed continue to have, a truly global resonance and acceptance, and have been considered worthy of being retained as part of respective social and moral code(s). The Ramayana encapsulates a moral framework that guides individuals in terms of navigating the complexities of human life through the example of Lord Ram who is unrelenting in his commitment to Dharma (duty and virtue) even in the face of adversity.

The association of the Ramayana, as an ancient Hindu epic, with "culture" rather than "religion" so far has been quite deliberate. The Ramayana is most certainly born of Hinduism—the religion. But as it travelled outside India via traders, travellers, and chroniclers, it became unmoored from ritual and deity. It came to embody the most pristine form of the oft-quoted iteration of Hinduism as "a way of life". The Ramayana understood in this vein is not merely a text. It is a cultural code that is based on a form of social organisation and exchange unique in its ability to deal with diversity. Divergences between retellings of the Ramayana across Asia therefore carry a productive friction that shows how an overarching set of moral ideals can adjust for internal differences and local conditions without causing a diminishing of the overarching category. To my mind, Indian philosophers whose treatise on humanism most closely resembled such thinking were Rabindranath Tagore[9] and Swami Vivekananda. To quote the latter's famous speech in Chicago in 1893: "I am proud to belong to a religion which has taught the world both tolerance and universal acceptance. We believe not only in universal toleration, but we accept all religions as true…As the different streams having their sources in different paths which men take through different tendencies, various though they appear, crooked or straight, all lead to Thee".[10]

Ordinarily, popularly practiced liberal ethics in modern-day politics denies the place of culture, promulgates the prominence of the state as the end of human evolution, and seeks to secularise the nature of its peoples. While in principle this seems like a neat method to erase diversity, thereby accommodating it, in reality it falters on many accounts. Secularism, while desirable in the function of the state, does not replace the force of culture in shaping human beings. Now some may indeed argue that secularism is intended to act as the religion of state, whereas other religions can be precluded to the realm of personal subjectivity. But this distinction between the state and the private sphere does not hold, at least not in a deliberative democracy. It is also based on an erroneous interpretation of man's need for community and the role that culture plays in providing a sense of belonging, history, and identity. In response, the Ramayana's global history is immersed in the tradition of embracing culture as a source of identity and inspiration without reducing it to narrow communal grooves. Culture can represent pride and strength in one's individuality, whether as a nation or a person, without shutting them off to cross-cultural learning, dialogue, and diversity. It is for this reason that the Ramayana "consists of multiplicities and pluralities; a lineage that implicitly permits questioning, elaboration, extension and elision within a convention of prescribed boundaries".[11]

A few housekeeping notes before I proceed: as an international relations scholar and historian, I write this book less as an expert on the Ramayana but more as a researcher of cultural ideas and their dissemination. As Asia begins to assert its prominence on the global stage, I am deeply interested in "who she was" and "what she can become" outside the tired and shackled framings and shibboleths of European lore. Moreover, all references to the Ramayana in this book are meant to signify a general reference to the ancient Hindu epic rather than any particular source of origin, iteration, or author. The first part of this book is structured to move from one Asian country to another, while uncovering the stories of how the Ramayana was localised, its unique interpretations and significances, how these developed over time, and what this tells us about how these peoples saw Hindu India. The second part of the book will reflect on what type of cultural globalisation the Ramayana represented, the reasons behind its continued significance, and its potential as an instrument of soft power for Rising India. In doing so, I have mainly relied on secondary sources and English translations available in academic and popular writings, aggregated them, and presented them to the reader in a lucid and accessible format. The choice of time frames and length is specific to each chapter, the country under study, and the relevance of the Ramayana to key moments in its cultural history.

Chapter 1

Thailand and The Ramakien

"Nothing else of Hindu origin has more profoundly affected the tone of Thai life than Ramayana".

—S.N. Desai[12]

In Thailand, the Ramayana is referred to as "Ramakien" and is the official national epic of the country. Remarkably, the region even had a capital city called Ayutthaya (from Ayodhya), and its lineage of kings since the 18th Century have derived their names from Ram (the current monarch is titled Rama IX)".[13] The ruins of Ayutthaya (now a UNESCO heritage site) and the Yala caves retell the story of the Ramayana across 178 giant murals, painted in the 18th Century. It was King Rama I of the Chakri dynasty who first composed the Thai version of the Hindu epic in 52,086 verses, influenced partly from Buddhist missionaries and their versions of the Dasharatha Jataka Tales of Lord Buddha, Valmiki's Ramayana, the Vishnu Purana and The Hanuman Nataka. Although King Rama I, as an avowed Buddhist, stated in the epilogue that The Ramakien should be read with traditional Buddhist tales, it remains an admixture of Hindu and Buddhist interpretations.[14] The Ramakien has significantly influenced the cultural, religious, and artistic landscape of Thailand, leaving an indelible mark on the country's society and politics. As a revered epic, it has been transmitted through oral traditions, literature, dance, art, and puppet theatre (Nang Yai[15]), shaping the identity of diverse communities.

It is important to note that just like India, there isn't a single version of the Ramakien in Thailand: there is "the version of King Rama I, the local versions of the North (called Paramahien, Horaman, Prommachak, and Lankasibho), the local versions of the Northeast (called PralakPralam, Praram Jataka, and Kwai Tuarapee), and the local versions of the South and the West consisting of Ban Kuankaey version, Wat Tha-khae version, and Wat Khanon version".[16] This chapter will discuss how the Thai version of the epic, The Ramakien, has served as an important religious text, a source of inspiration for Thai art and literature, as well as a tool for political propaganda. In essence, The Ramakien is a testament to the enduring power of the Ramayana and its ability to inspire and influence people across cultures and borders.

There are some notable differences between conventional readings of The Valmiki Ramayana and The Ramakien, with the latter being more strongly influenced by the South Indian versions of the Ramayana, especially the Kamba Ramayana. There is a predictable influence of Thai culture on names, food, clothing, weaponry, customs, beliefs, and aesthetics. Lord Ram or "Phra Ram" is devoid of his divine characteristics and instead is portrayed as a Thai prince. Ravan or "Tosakanth," instead of having his heads severed and reunited with his body, it is his limbs that are the subject of magical prowess. His death is not brought about by Lord Ram's use of the Brahma-shastra on his naval. Instead, in the Thai version, Ravan's soul is kept safely guarded in a cage away from his physical body. It is only after Hanuman locates and crushes his soul between two big stones that Lord Ram is able to kill Ravan on the battlefield.[17] There is also the introduction of new characters and episodes, such as the king of the nether world Maiyarab, who is said to have kidnapped Lord Ram. He is subsequently rescued by the heroics of Hanuman.[18]

More importantly however, Ravan in comparison to Lord Ram enjoys more prominence and experiences a nuanced portrayal rather than being shown as evil incarnate. As A.K. Ramanujan has argued in his essay "300 Ramayanas", The Ramakien notes "Ravana's resourcefulness and learning, while his abduction of Sita is seen as an act of love and is viewed with sympathy. The Thais are moved by Ravana's sacrifice of family, kingdom and life itself for the sake of a woman. Unlike Valmiki's characters, the Thai ones are a fallible, human mixture of good and evil. The fall of Ravana here makes one sad. It is not an occasion for unambiguous rejoicing, as it is in Valmiki".[19] Ravan has a statue dedicated to him in the centre of Bangkok, near the Grand Palace at the Temple of the Emerald Buddha (Wat Phra Kaew). The depiction of his death too is not traditionally performed as part of folk theatre as it is considered inauspicious.[20]

The Ramakien's interpretation of "Nang Sida" or Sita's birth is also strikingly different, indicating that she could be born of Ravan's wife Mandodari, after the latter had consumed "a blessed rice ball" stolen from King Dasaratha (in the Valmiki version it is porridge). As the story goes, Ravan discards Sita after it is prophesied that she will cause the downfall of his kingdom. But the sea goddess protects her and takes her to King Janaka. Sita's banishment at the end of the epic also takes a dramatic turn, as the demoness Surpanakha—who had had earlier been mutilated by Lord Ram and Lakshman in the forest—enters Sita's service as a maid and entices her into drawing a picture of Ravan and leaving it under Ram's bed, causing question's related to Sita's infidelity.[21] It takes the persuasion of God Shiva to bring Sita back from the bowels of Mother Earth and to reunite her with Lord Ram on Mount Kailasa. This is contrastingly happy ending in comparison to The Valmiki Ramayana. Although Lord Ram is an incarnation of God Vishnu, he is considered a human figure and subordinate to god Shiva. The focus on "War," instead of family values and sacrifice, is also noticeably prominent in the Thai version, signifying its relatability to early Thai history that was quite conflict ridden.[22] Finally, Hanuman is not depicted as devout or a celibate. A detailed study of 39 deviations from The Valmiki Ramayana are examined by S. Singaravelu in his classic essay and can be referred to for further details.[23]

Various places in Thailand also owe their names and significance to The Ramakien. Bangkok is still referred to as Ayutthaya popularly. A town called "Lopburi to the north of Bangkok is named after Lord Ram's son "Luv". A flat top area on a mountain called "Khao Sanphaya" near Lopburi is believed to have been created by Hanuman's tail being wrapped around. The waters of the "Thale Chup Son" lake are considered sacred because it is believed Lord Ram once immersed his arrows in the lake. Thai king Mongkut in 1854 had his weapons sprinkled with the waters of the lake so that they may be blessed for the same reason.[24]

The Ramakien had a significant impact on Thai art and

literature, in particular based on King Rama II's adaption with fewer episodes offered the potential for more dramatic performances. Since then, the Hindu epic has been a source of inspiration for Thai artists and writers for centuries. The characters and stories of The Ramakien have been depicted in Thai art and literature in various forms, including murals, sculptures, and paintings. The Ramakien has also been adapted into various forms of Thai literature, including poetry, drama, and novels such as the "Lakhon text," Phraya Mahanuphab's "Nirat" poem, the "Kham Phak Ramakien" and "Bot LakhonRamakien"—both literary texts dealing with specific parts of the legend. References to Lord Ram are also found in other literary texts such as the "Kloong Prakat Chaeng Nam" which was composed during the period of King Uthong or Ramadhipati I (1351–1369 C.E.)".[25] It has also had a significant impact on Thai dance-drama and has been adapted into various forms, including Khon, Lakhon Nai, and Nang Yai. "Khon" is a form of masked dance-drama that is performed mainly for the Thai royalty and aristocracy, depicting scenes relating to "the abduction of Rama by the demon Maiyarab (Mahi Ravana), Hanuman's journey to Lanka in search of Sita and the fire ordeal of Sita".[26] It enjoyed particular prominence during the reign of Rama VI.[27] As S.R. Praveen writes for The Hindu: "back in those days, it was performed only by members of the royal family, with the audience too from the upper classes. Performed with elaborate costumes and sets, it is still performed under royal patronage, but with the doors open to the larger public, both as performers and the audience. The Ramakien continues to be the major source material".[28] However, some popular folk traditions did evolve to incorporate elements of the Ramayana, such as the "Nang Yai" which is a form of shadow puppetry and predates the "Khon".

The Ramakien also played a significant role in Thai politics. The Thai monarchy has translated The Ramakien periodically as part of national lore to legitimise its rule and to reinforce the idea of the divine right of kings. The Thai version of the epic portrays Lord Ram as a just and righteous king who embodies the ideals of the perfect ruler. The Thai monarchy has identified itself with Ram, and The Ramakien has been used to reinforce the idea that the Thai king rule through divine ordinance. The Ramakien has thus been used as a tool for political ends. For instance, during the reign of King Rama IX, the Ramakien was used to promote the idea of national unity and to reinforce the Thai nation as a single entity. It was used to promote the idea of the Thai monarchy as a unifying force that could bring together the different ethnic groups in Thailand.[29] Unlike India in the Nehruvian era, which sought to overcome social fissures through the secularisation of politics, in Thailand it was The Ramakien and its spiritual influence that was used to bridge ethnic divides.

Scholars have identified this as the key reason behind The Ramakien's prominence in Thai society and politics. Srisurang Poolthupya argues that The Ramakien inspires "virtues and loyalty". Therefore, it was a useful and powerful instrument for Thai rulers to mobilise support for their institutions of governance. Due to the parallels between Hindu philosophy with Buddhist pre-existing iconography and textual elements, this did not contradict any of the peoples existing spiritual sensibilities. The "cult of the god king" receives emphasis in the Thai version. For instance, after the defeat of Ravan, Lord Ram gifts half the kingdom

Chapter 2

Cambodia and The Reamker

The Ramayana has transcended geographical and cultural boundaries to become a significant cultural touchstone in various parts of Southeast Asia. Among these, Cambodia stands out as a nation profoundly influenced by the Ramayana. This chapter aims to explore the multifaceted impact of the Ramayana on Cambodian culture, art, religion, and society. From the architectural marvels of Angkor Wat to the performing arts and religious rituals, the text has greatly influenced Cambodia, shaping its cultural identity and fostering a unique blend of Hindu and Buddhist traditions. Although the original geographical setting of the text in India and general storyline was retained, the Khmer version also has significant changes. As Saveros Pau describes it, the Ramayana in Cambodia "was made of a Valmikian warp into which Khmer authors wove a gamut of weft-yarns drawn from their Buddhist culture".[33] It has been noted that in Cambodia, the earliest known evidence of the Ramayana was from a Sanskrit inscription and a sculpture of Lord Ram in the Takeo province dated to the 6th century.[34]

In Cambodia, the earliest evidence of the Ramayana's presence dates back to the 7th century and the reign of King Jayavarman I. The transmission of the Ramayana to Hanuman. But Hanuman is unable to share the burden of the throne and relinquishes the same to Lord Ram. While The Ramakien teaches loyalty, it also imposes some characteristics on Thai royals to be ideal kings in the image of Lord Ram, such as to rule righteously and to seek the counsel of his ministers.[30]

The cultural heritage of The Ramakien is somewhat diminishing in present-day Thailand. Since popular expressions of The Ramakien were mainly performed for the Thai aristocracy and royalty and did not permeate Thai society at large, there isn't much resonance with the popular masses anymore. Thai people are certainly aware of The Ramakien but lack an emotive or interpersonal connection beyond the Royal Court. In addition, Thai youths have shown lesser inclination to join troupes and continue the heritage of their forefathers as performers. Although the Thai Government has sought to patronise art forms related to The Ramakien, including providing subsidies to performers at the National Theatre, the effect of these efforts has been unclear. One of the most prominent troupes called the "Joe Louis Puppet Theatre" was struggling with financial issues and had to focus on alternative stories to The Ramakien in order to attract audiences.[31] It would seem that The Ramakien's survival in Thailand will be directly linked to the ebbs and flows of the popularity and influence of the Thai Royal family. It is worthwhile to note that a special logo selected by the King Bhumibol Adulyadej at the occasion of completion of sixty years of his accession to the throne in 2006 shows his throne being protectively flanked by Hanuman and Sugriv, two prominent characters from the Ramakien and protectors of Lord Ram.[32]

to Cambodia can be traced to the trade and cultural exchanges between India and Southeast Asia during this period. However, it was under the rule of the Khmer Empire, particularly during the Angkor period (9th to 15th centuries), that the Ramayana gains prominence in Cambodian society. In Cambodia, the Ramayana is called the "Rāmakerti" (glory of Ram) and is also locally known as "The Reamker". It has undergone various adaptations that reflect the cultural nuances of the Khmer people, and is considered incomplete due to omissions such as the death of Ravan. As Trent Walker has highlights, "the most famous version, Reamker I: Early Episodes, is also the oldest extant recension, having been composed in Middle Khmer during the sixteenth or seventeenth centuries... Much of the remaining narrative is found only in the eighteenth-century text Reamker II: Later Episodes".[35] These two volumes of The Reamker are said to have been composed anonymously by at least 3 authors between the 16th and 19th Century. To manage the unwieldy nature of The Valmiki Ramayana, The Reamker offers a compressed version with selective tales and are incomplete versions of the original.

The Reamker shares the core narrative of the Hindu epic but incorporates distinct elements that resonate with Cambodian sensibilities. Notable differences include the portrayal of certain characters, the addition of local folklore, and the infusion of moral lessons that align with Khmer cultural values. To make the figure of Lord Ram compatible with Buddhist tenets, he was made to resemble Prince Siddhartha, and subsequently as an object of veneration and sacred. Unlike the Thai version that emphasises war and martial valour, Lord Ram is seen as engaging with his enemies with tactful arguments, moral counsel, and only reluctantly with battle in a "non-violent way" wherein his magical powers were able to neutralise the fighting devices of demons. Lord Ram also noted as giving deceased warriors such as Bali (Peali) a proper royal funeral. As the pre-eminent translator of The Reamker, Judith Jacob, has argued, "The reverence with which Cambodians regard the character of Ram is not merely for the original Indian reason, that he is a god, living on earth in order to quell evil. In the Reamker Rama is presented as being more than that: he is the Buddha himself".[36] However, despite this Lord Ram is also shown to embody human desires, daily conflicts, jealousy, and marital tensions. His war with Ravan is not merely a divine mission, but is also party driven by such human instincts.

The monkeys in Lord Ram's army, including Hanuman, are shown in a poor light as ugly and mischievous creatures, mainly due to their reputation in Khmer culture "for being too noisy, restless, inquisitive, mischievous, and sly, if not vicious—in brief, prone to troublemaking".[37] To accommodate this divergence between the understanding of monkeys in Khmer culture and their prominence in the Ramayana, "Monkeys were given therein two faces. The first one, foreign to Khmer culture, was a composite of high moral values, a capability to see right and wrong and then to choose the good cause, an unquestioning loyalty and devotion to their masters, a martial skill tinged with magic, and, to crown all this, a physical attraction and beauty! The second one derived from all the traits, physical and moral, that Khmer people had always attributed to them since time immemorial".[38] The story of Sita's birth is also different: King Janaka was ploughing the fields with his royal oxen and golden plough near the Yamuna when "there suddenly appeared a divine, golden maiden on a raft, herself in a magnificent lotus-flower, completely perfect, of superlative and remarkable splendour. The king was highly delighted with this, a royal daughter".[39] There are also more trivial changes. For instance, in The Valmiki Ramayana, when the god of fire (*Agni*) attends Sita's "*svayamvara*" he is shown riding a ram (bighorn sheep). But this animal was not native to Cambodia. Hence in The Reamker, the god of fire is portrayed as riding a rhinoceros owing to the animal's fierce nature.

The most iconic representation of The Reamker in Cambodia is undoubtedly the Angkor Wat temple complex, a UNESCO World Heritage site. Constructed during the 12th century by King Suryavarman II, Angkor Wat is dedicated to the Hindu god Vishnu. Here Vishnu, often depicted in various forms, coexists with Buddha statues, creating a unique spiritual ambiance that transcends rigid religious boundaries. The temple's bas-reliefs vividly depict scenes from The Reamker, illustrating the epic's central characters, events, and moral teachings. This is particularly visible in "The Bayon Temple", built during the reign of king Jayavarman VII. The southern gallery of Angkor Wat is adorned with intricate carvings that narrate the Ramayana's essential episodes. The Battle of Lanka, Hanuman's leap across the ocean, and Lord Ram's triumph over Ravan are meticulously etched into the sandstone walls, showcasing the Khmer artisans' unparalleled craftsmanship. The temple's alignment with the cardinal points of the compass is believed to symbolise the cosmic significance of The Reamker, reinforcing the epic's spiritual and metaphysical dimensions. Khmer sculptors were inspired by the epic as far back as the Sambor Prei Kuk period during the 8th century. Everyday items too carried the Ramayana's imprint: "names of trees or plants are, for example, based on characters in the Rāmāyana. For instance, LambaeNbrahRāma, the "javelin of Rāma," is a kind of orchid; Doh nāN Setā, "the breasts of Sītā," is also a kind of orchid; and SramaPiphek, "VibhisanaSrama fruit".[40]

The Reamker's influence also extends beyond the static carvings of Angkor Wat and finds dynamic expression in Cambodia's traditional performing arts. The classical dance-drama known as "Robam Tep Apsara" often incorporates episodes from The Reamker, with dancers adorned in elaborate costumes and headdresses that mirror the celestial beings depicted in the Hindu epic. Through graceful movements and intricate choreography, Cambodian dancers bring the characters of The Reamker to life, captivating audiences and preserving a centuries-old tradition. The subject of the traditional shadow play ("spaekdham") with puppets is also exclusively based on The Reamker. The popular masked dance, lkhonkhol, which has become associated with the cult of local deities, was based on certain episodes of The Reamker. There is often a snake like portrayal in Cambodian dance moves. As Cambodian scholar and former minister of culture Nouth Narang explains:

> "the Cambodian version of the Ramayana dance drama and all other Khmer dances are based on the movement of the "*naga*", the snake, because we believe that our grandparents are the "*naga*", king's stock. So, our dance follows the movements of the "naga", or snake, which are graceful loops or spirals. It is very important to

> remember this because whether it is the Apsara dance, the dance by the heavenly court dancers, or the dances depicting scenes from the Indian epic, the Ramayana, the movements are basically of the loops and spirals that embody the movement of the snake".[41]

There is quite a lot of emphasis on costumes as well and dancers have to spend hours before performances for them to be stitched on by a couturier. Silversmiths create opulent sampots, or skirts woven from gold and silver thread, as well as a wide range of belts and designs. Reamker figures are known for their highly decorated headdresses, which have themes evocative of architectural ornamentation patterns. This is seen in the crown's pyramid-like formations and the ornaments' triple arrangement.[42] Ultimately, whether performed on the stage or recited in village festivals, the Reamker remains one of the most beloved pieces of classical literature in contemporary Cambodia. In fact, an episode from The Reamker is performed in Cambodian villages if there is a shortfall of rain. The episode is of Kumbhakaran (Ravan's brother) blocking the supply of water for Lord Ram's army of monkeys by sleeping across a river in his enlarged form, and Hanuman and Angad succeeding in releasing the water thereafter by using magical tricks.

Finally, in Cambodia too The Reamker has played a role in political power representations. Sophearith Siyonn's study of the Ramayana in ancient Cambodia explores the political aspects of the Hindu epic, showing how it was used to weave together different aspects of life, forming and constantly evolving narrative. The epic has been used to legitimize political power and authority. As Sophearith Siyonn writes, "The battle between Rāma and Rāvana was often compared to the battle between Khmer kings and neighbouring kings. Noticeably, during the reign of King Jayavarman VII, the selected episodes were obviously matched to particular events and people". He continues: "It is the Rāmāyana which, perhaps more than anything else (ritual, narrative, doctrinal texts...) manages to weave together these different aspects of life forming and constantly re-forming Khmer society".[43] However, this was a two-way process. Not only was the Ramayana used to "exalt the kings and impart the message to the people to behave properly and to abide by the law," but its narrative and its prevalence also maintained a check on the "abuse of royal power or unethical behaviour". In short, the Hindu epic represented "dharma" or aspirational moral quantities for both, the peoples of Cambodia as well as its royal order.[44]

Chapter 3

Indonesia and The Kakawin Ramayana

The Ramayana has exerted a profound and enduring influence on the cultural, literary, religious, and artistic landscape of Indonesia. This chapter embarks on a detailed exploration of the multifaceted impact of the Ramayana in Indonesia, navigating through historical connections, literary adaptations, artistic expressions, religious implications, societal impact, the contemporary relevance of the timeless Hindu epic. The Ramayana has had a profound influence on Indonesian culture, particularly among the Javanese and Balinese communities, serving as a moral guide and a form of artistic expression. Trade, culture and war brought the Hindu epic to Indonesia at the apogee of Buddhism in Sumatra, West, and Central Java around the 8th or 9th century during the Medang Kingdom (732–1006 AD). The bas-reliefs of Ramayana and Krishnayana scenes are carved on balustrades of the 9th century Prambanan temple in Yogyakarta, as well as in the 14th century Penataran temple in East Java.

However, its literary version, which came to be known as the "Kakawin Ramayana," was penned by Yogiswara in kakawin meter in the old Javanese language almost a century later.[45] There was thereafter a "Kakawin Arjunawijaya", a branch tale of the Ramayana that was later reworked by the great court poet Tantular during the reign of Yasadipura I (1729–1780 CE) as the Sera Aijuna Sasrabau. Finally, in the 18th century, "the court in Central Java sponsored a return to the Valmiki literary tradition in the Serat Rama—a fresh interpretation of the Old Javanese classic".[46] Overall, as a literary corpus, The Kakawin Ramayana has deeply influenced Indonesian culture, and various versions of the Ramayana (over 1200 by some accounts) have been adapted to local contexts, reflecting the text's ability to exceed the boundaries of religion and ethnicity.

The Kakawin Ramayana was most prominent in the pre-modern city of Bali, which is still a majority Hindu part of Indonesia. In fact, "in Bali, the story of Rama still plays a central part in the religious and cultural life of the island, and in the twentieth century became a popular subject for illustrated palm-leaf manuscripts". It was also re-written in modern Javanese and popularised in Java during "the late 18th-century renaissance of literature at the central Javanese courts of Surakarta and Yogyakarta".[47] In terms of The Kakawin Ramayana's influence on the historical sites of Indonesia, "the first portrayal of the Ramayana on stone was seen in Central Java, where the epic was carved onto the courtyard balustrades in the Chandi Shiva and Chandi Brahma temples, locally known as Lara Jonggrang. Lara Jonggrang, also has the glory of holding a full pictorial representation of the Ramayan (Balakanda to Uttarakanda). Interestingly, the town closest to this temple is known as Yogyakarta, which in old Javanese means Ayodhya (Ram's birthplace)".[48] Historical representations of The Kakawin

Ramayana are also prominent in the city of Sumatra. In Indonesia as a whole however, as Helen Creese has argued, "from its earliest renderings on palm leaf and stone, it served as a source of political, strategic and moral guidance for rulers and as the inspiration for generations of poets, artisans and performers".[49]

It is believed that the source of the first half of the old Javanese Kakawin Ramayana, instead of The Valmiki Ramayana, was possibly the Sanskrit poem *Bhattikavya* written by Indian poet Bhatti around the 6–7th century AD, as it is almost identical in its rendering. But the second half of the Kakawin Ramayana is independent in relation to other Indian versions of the Hindu epic and may have been influenced by the popular circulation of oral histories of the Ramayana at the time. For instance, the second half of the Kakawin Ramayana introduces a Javanese guardian demigod to the story, called *Dhayana*, (regarded as the god of Java Semar or Twalen in Balinese literature) and his four sons called the four Punokawan or "clown servants". These characters are most popular and have gained notoriety in theatrical representations and shadow puppetry such as the Wayang performances.

Sita is shown in the Kakawin Ramayana as a fierce, bold, and assertive character. She even attempts to fight the Asuras (demons) instead of waiting for Lord Ram to save her from Lanka. Thus, "it is not uncommon in Indonesian Wayang performances to see Sita's character being played with her chin and head up in a defiant position".[50] Sita's fabled bow is also "not that of Shiva, but a magical reincarnation of the placenta of her birth" due to the placenta's prominence in Javanese mythology. Due to the popularity of written expression of love in pre-modern Java, when Hanuman visits Sita in the Lankan gardens, she "writes a passionate letter" to Lord Ram. Sita's loyal companion in captivity, Trijata, also denounces Lord Ram at the end of the epic when he doubts her loyalty. This too was in line with the "intelligent and articulate" companions of women in Indonesian royalty.[51]

Hanuman is a much-revered character and is described as white monkey who has mystical powers and single-handedly overpowers Ravan's army of demons. He figures in many of the Hindu temples and archaeological sites in Indonesia depicting episodes from The Kakawin Ramayana. In a socio-cultural sense there is particular emphasis on "the function (duty, dharma) of the king as a Kshatriya was to fight and maintain the "welfare of the world", to defend and promote order and prosperity".[52] For instance, Ravan's brother Kumbhakarna is portrayed as a follower of "dharma" as he fights in defence of his homeland despite vehemently disagreeing with the morality of Ravan's abduction of Sita.[53] Ravan's other brother Vibhishana also has prominence. After taking over Lanka's throne he delivers the *"Astabrat"* (eight vows), which is considered the most influential passage in Javanese Ramayana literature detailing the ideal conduct of a king.[54] As Soewito Santoso argues, "the teachings of Rama to Wibisana have been adhered to by the Javanese kings of Surakarta and Yogyakarta, and at present are still contemplated as effective guidance in statemanship by the politicians and office bearers in Indonesia".[55]

The Kakawin Ramayana has greatly shaped the cultural landscape of Indonesia and its influence can be traced through various art forms, literature, dance, and religious practices. One of the most iconic forms of Indonesian art influenced by the Kakawin Ramayana is the "WayangKulit". This traditional Javanese shadow puppetry, which starts after the harvest season and continues until the monsoons. brings the Hindu epic to life through intricate leather puppets, manipulated by skilled puppeteers. The stories of the Kakawin Ramayana are performed in night-long shows, captivating audiences with the timeless tales. Wayang puppetry has ensured that the Kakawin Ramayana became embedded in the cultural matrix of Indonesia. Prominent puppet theatres in Indonesia – Wayang Golek (wooden rod-puppet play) of the Sundanese and the WayangKulit (leather shadow-puppet play) of the Javanese and Balinese—draw much of their repertoire from The Kakawin Ramayana.

The Balinese Kecak dance also portrays The Kakawin Ramayana. The performance famously has a fire show depicting the burning of Lanka by Hanuman. Dancers playing the roles of Rama, Sita, Lakhsmana, Jatayu, Hanuman, Ravana, Kumbhakarna and Indrajit are surrounded by a troupe of over 50 bare-chested men who serve as the chorus chanting "cak". Similarly, in Yogyakarta, the Wayang Wong Javanese dance retells Ramayana through the famous Ramayana Ballet performed on the Trimurti Prambanan open-air stage, with the renowned Prambanan temple as the backdrop. The Kakawin Ramayana has not only influenced the arts but has also become intertwined with religious practices in Indonesia. The Hindu epic has been embraced by communities on the islands of Java and Bali, where it coexists with other Indonesian beliefs and traditions. This syncretism is evident in the construction of temples, such as Prambanan in Central Java, adorned with reliefs depicting scenes from the Ramayana. The Kakawin Ramayana serves as a cultural unifier in Indonesia, transcending religious and ethnic boundaries. It is not confined to Hindu communities but is celebrated and embraced by Indonesian peoples of diverse religious backgrounds. This shared cultural heritage fosters a sense of national identity, contributed to the unity of the Indonesian archipelago.

As Indonesia was Islamised, the Ramayana was retained by the Sufi-influenced Javanese court in the Perso-Arabic tradition and "popular deities and heroes of the Hindu past transformed into historical heroes, albeit extraordinary ones, who were seen as the ancestors of the Javanese kings".[56] The great Indonesian Sufi saint Sunan Kalijaga, who brought Islam to Java, was also popularly credited with delivering the Ramayana (having ostensibly being informed of the text as a set of compiled stories by Yudhishthira as the tale goes). Hindu gods were substituted: Lord Ram was denied as an incarnation of Vishnu and the gifts of Ravan are inherited through "Nabi Adam", an agent of Allah. And when the Dutch colonisers challenged Indonesian unity, such retellings of episodes from the Ramayana were used to quell dissent in the royal family and reconcile warring states. There was also a later interation of the Ramayana in Indonesia called the "Serat Kanda," which also has equally fantastical deviations from The Valmiki Ramayana. As Indonesia continues to evolve, the Ramayana, with all its iterations, remains a source of inspiration, connecting the past with the present and fostering a sense of shared identity amongst its diverse population.

Chapter 4

Malaysia and The Hikayat Seri Rama

One region where the influence of the Ramayana is profoundly evident is Malaysia. This chapter explores the multifaceted impact of the Ramayana on Malaysia, examining its historical roots, cultural integration, and religious significance: from the early waves of Indian migration to the contemporary manifestations in Malaysian society. The Ramayana has played a pivotal role in shaping the cultural landscape of this Southeast Asian nation. The historical connection between India and Malaysia dates back to ancient times when Indian traders and merchants traversed the maritime routes, establishing trade links with the Malay Archipelago. The migration of Indians to the Malay Peninsula brought with it not only spices and goods but also cultural and religious elements, including the Ramayana. The early Indian settlers in Malaysia, mainly Tamils, played a crucial role in introducing the epic to the local population. Scholars have found that there are deep resonances between the Malaysian Ramayana or the Hikayat Seri Rama and Tamil folklore.[57] The Hikayat Seri Rama, through oral traditions and performances, became an integral part of the Malaysian cultural landscape. As the

Indian diaspora took root in Malaysia, they brought their customs, rituals, and stories, embedding the Ramayana into the social fabric of Malaysian society.

The Hikayat Seri Rama represents a significant cultural and literary synthesis, as it adapts the Hindu epic into a form that resonated with Malay-speaking audiences. Hikayat is an Arabic word that literally translates to "stories" and is a popular form of Malay literature. The roots of the Hikayat Seri Rama can be traced back to the early centuries of the Common Era when Indian cultural and religious influence began to permeate the Malay Archipelago. Over time, stories such as the Hikayat Seri Rama were orally transmitted and adapted to suit the cultural context of the Malay world. The initial transmission of the Ramayana in the Malay world was likely through storytelling. Griots, or traditional storytellers, played a crucial role in narrating the adventures of Rama, Sita, and Hanuman to local audiences. This oral tradition allowed for a certain degree of flexibility and adaptation, enabling the incorporation of local elements into the narrative. As the influence of Islam grew in Malaysia, this adaptation involved not only linguistic changes but also a recontextualization of the story within the framework of Islam. The Hikayat Seri Rama exists in manuscript form too, and the earliest known manuscripts Hikayat Seri Rama are believed to have been written between the 13th and 15th centuries. One of the oldest Malay manuscripts in this country – and probably the oldest known illuminated Malay manuscript – is a copy of the Hikayat Seri Rama now held in the Bodleian Library, Oxford, which was in the possession of Archbishop Laud in 1635.[58] These manuscripts were handwritten and meticulously illustrated, reflecting the importance of the

Hindu epic in the cultural and religious consciousness of the Malay society.

Unlike the Valmiki Ramayana, the Hikayat Seri Rama is written in Arabic and reflects Islamic ethics. Richard Winstedt argues that the text was finalized in the Kingdom of Malacca, "which was still conservative enough to like the old tales of the Hindu period, provided that they were presented in a form which Muslim pundits could condone".[59] The characters, including Lord Ram, Sita, and Hanuman, are presented as virtuous figures whose actions align with Islamic values and themes of justice, loyalty, and the consequences of moral choices. As Shekhar Sen points out in his review of Harry Aveling's translation of the Hikayat Seri Rama, as Hindu and Buddhist influence waned in South-east Asia, by the early 16th century its Islamisation was almost complete. Interestingly, though the dominant religion changed, cultural traditions did not, but minor changes were brought in: "...the text was written down for a Muslim court... which was still conservative enough to like the old tales of the Hindu period, provided they were presented in a form which Muslim pundits could condone". The script of the Hikayat Seri Rama was Arabic and Allah replaced the Hindu gods. His Prophet was named Adam Nabi who is said to have blessed Ravan with his powers. Lord Ram is shown as a human character with failings of "arrogance and vanity". In fact, it is his brother Lakshman who is "given a greater role". Ravan is also praised for at least initially being "a noble, dynamic character" as he was rewarded by Allah with dominion over earth, air, water, and the nether world for his relentless practice of austerities.[60] As S. Singaravelu argues, "The Malay version and the Thai versions seem to give precedence to the story of Ravan's youth and his early deeds and achievements over that of Ram".[61]

There also other deviations: Sita asks Hanuman to pay his respects to the stone on which Nabi Adam landed on earth; the roots, leaves and bark of the tree planted by Nabi Adam were medicines to revive Lakshman; and King Dasharatha is described as Nabi Adam's great-grandson.[62] In the Hikayat Seri Rama, King Dasharatha, on the advice of Kaikeyi (mentioned as a concubine), anoints Bharat as his successor as Lord Ram is initially shown as mischievous.[63] The Manthara-Kaikeyi conspiracy is not mentioned. Sita is once again described as Ravan's daughter. Ravan is said to have asked King Dasharatha for the hand of his wife and Lord Ram's mother "Mandu-dari". However, Mandu-dari deceived Ravan and instead sends a replica "Mandu-daki" with him to Lanka. Sita is born of Ravan and Mandu-daki. Later, as Ravan's brother Vibhishana prophecies that Sita would be the cause of his downfall, Ravan abandons her in a jewel box in the ocean, where she is found by King Janaka. Based on these retellings, it would seem that the Hikayat Seri Rama is inspired by Sanghadasa'sVasudevahindi and the Adbhut Ramayana and has no compunctions about ad-hoc borrowing from the Thai, Cambodian and Javanese tellings.

Notably, in the Hikayat Seri Rama, Hanuman is Lord Ram's son. As the story goes, after Lord Ram and Sita bathe in an enchanted pond, "Sita spews a jewel from her mouth which Baya Bata [*Pavana*] flies away with and puts in the open mouth of [*Anjana*], who then gives birth to Hanuman, an ape with a human head, ears adorned with earrings". This version is entirely unique in South East Asia.

Another novelty is Sita's role in Ravan's death. She discloses to Hanuman that if one can "smite the small head 'as big as a candle-nut' behind his right ear and steal the enchanted sword from Mandu-daki…[Ravan] will not die but will be unable to stand up". This method is then deployed by Lord Ram to defeat Ravan, although the latter's death is clouded in some mystery. In the Hikayat Seri Rama, Lord Ram does not return to Ayodhya either. Instead he stays as ruler of Lanka before retiring to a hermitage and spending forty years with Sita, Lakshman, and Hanuman before dying of old age. There are several other minor deviations as well such as: Ravan as peacemaker among his fighting relatives; Lord Ram slaying great monsters and subduing four angry princes; the conflict between Maharishi Mahaganta and the rakshasa king Jaya Sang; Lord Ram's army defeating Jaya Sang's relatives; Hanuman's amorous escapades [a total deviation from Indian tradition]; Mula Matani's battle; the *Lakshman-rekha*; Sita's first son and how she is magically gifted a second son; Badayasa's battle (Bhashmalochana of Krittivas) etc".[64]

Traditional dance forms and dramas based on the Ramayana, such as Mak Yong and Wayang Kulit, usually include episodes or prominent characters. These performances serve as a medium for cultural expression and storytelling. In particular, the Ramayana has had a profound influence on Malaysian shadow puppetry, in the traditional art form known as Wayang Kulit. Wayang Kulit involves the use of intricately carved leather puppets, which are manipulated behind a backlit screen by a puppeteer. This traditional performing art has been a popular form of entertainment and cultural expression in Malaysia, and the

Ramayana serves as a major source for the narratives enacted in Wayang Kulit performances. Traditional music and chants accompany Wayang Kulit performances, enhancing the storytelling experience. With its emphasis on morality, duty, and righteousness, the Ramayana provides a foundation for exploring ethical themes in the Wayang Kulit. Performances may highlight moral lessons and ethical dilemmas faced by the characters, contributing to the educational and cultural aspects of the art form. Ghulam-Sarwar Yousof argues that the "the main sources of dramatic repertoire for the Malaysian shadow play, wayangkulit Kelantan, are the literary Hikayat Seri Rama and the oral Hikayat Maharaja Wana with some influences from the Patani version of the epic from southern Thailand".[65] In terms of historical sites, the Batu Caves in Malaysia depict several chapters from the Ramayana, further demonstrating its Tamil ancestry.[66]

The Hikayat Seri Rama continues further to include the birth of Lord Ram's sons, Lava and Kusa, and ends with the descent of Sita into the earth and the ascent of Lord Ram to heaven. It ends with the following words:

> "This concludes the story of Seri Rama, a brave and heroic king, unequalled in all the world. His greatness was a gift from God, who wants all his servants to be happy and free from danger. God, All-Glorious and All-Mighty, generously gives us many gifts. When you read this Hikayat, I ask you not to be too harsh. Mankind is full of mistakes and prone to forgetfulness. There is only One who never makes any mistakes".[67]

Chapter 5

Laos and The Phra Lak Phra Ram

The Ramayana or "The Phra Lak Phra Ram" is the national epic of the Laotian peoples, and is named after its two principal characters, named after two principal characters, Phra Lak, or Lakshman and Phra Ram, or Lord Ram. At times it is also referred to as "Phra Ram sadok" (Ram Jataka).[68] This is because it is more heavily influenced by Buddhist interpretations rather than Sanskrit versions such as The Valmiki Ramayana. Since Laos is a Theravada Buddhist country, the Ramayana is not associated with Hinduism, but is instead rendered as a Jataka Story (Dasharatha Jataka), or a recounting of the Buddha's previous lives. For instance, Lord Ram is considered a previous avatar of Lord Buddha and is accordingly regarded as the epitome of moral leadership and an unrelenting follower of his dharma. Similarly, Raphanasuan or Ravan, is considered a previous incarnation of the demon Mara, who had tried to block Lord Buddha's ascent to enlightenment. Interestingly, the Laotian text also changes the geographical setting and the epic takes place along the Mekong River (referred to as the "mother of waters" in Buddhist folklore of the Tai tribes) and its tributaries from Vientiane down to Savannakhet, rather than the Ganges. As the official website of the Royal Palace Museum Theatre in Laos states:

> The Lao Ramayana differs from the original Indian version of the Ramayana. The Ramayana reached Laos late, around the sixteenth century, brought by Buddhist missions. The original Indian epic adapted to the geography, names of figures and regional languages. Consequently, all the story in the Lao Ramayana is situated in the valley of the Mekong, the grand royal city is called Chanthabouri Si Sattanak, while Lanka remains an island far from the heart of the kingdom, inaccessible and dangerous.[69]

The Mekong River is crucial to The Phra Lak Phra Ram, and like other Lao literary texts such as "Sin Sai," it spends considerable time detailing "a journey along valleys, woods, and rivers of Mekong's basin" and "the richness of the natural resources in Laos, such as the trees, fruits, and animals, both terrestrial and aquatic, and all minerals through frequent comparisons of descriptions as illustrated in the original story".[70] The names of places along the river in the text still corresponds to the names of real towns and tributaries along the Mekong River, as well as the surrounding ecology. It is conjectured that Laos itself was earlier known as "Lava", after the son of Lord Ram.[71] In terms of geographical markers, it is also noteworthy that certain places in Laos also get their name from the text. It is mentioned in an episode that Sita asks Hanuman to get her some mushrooms from Lanka. Since Hanuman fails to identify the particular variety of mushrooms desired by Sita, he uproots an entire mountain from Lanka and brings it to Luang Prabang in Laos. This is how Mount Phousi in Laos gets its name.[72] The transmission of the Ramayana to Laos, similar to Cambodia and Thailand, is rooted in historical connections through trade routes, cultural exchanges, and migration, and is believed to have occurred around the 8th or 9th Century. The spread of Indian culture from Thailand, the Cambodian Khmer kingdom (King Chenla Jayavarman I (657–681 A.D.) had occupied central and upper Laos) and the Malaysian Cham kingdom, including religious and literary traditions, trade and commerce – all contributed to the adoption of the Ramayana in Laos.

As often occurs in the localisation process of literary works, the Phra Lak Phra Ram has also been given a local flavour by means of setting it in the Lao milieu. Lord Ram is considered the son of Viruppakhah, the King of Jambudvipa, and instead Bali and Sugreva are considered sons of King Dasharatha – offering an almost equal importance in the narration of the text. Due to the latter's popularity, episodes from The Phra Lak Phra Ram are also combined with narrations of the Panchatantra (Nathan Nang Tantai). For instance, there is a story of a snake seeking refuge in a pond of frogs. When the frogs deny the snake's request, the latter narrates the story of Lord Ram to the frog king, explaining that despite Vibhishana being Ravan's brother, Lord Ram provided him with refuge. Therefore, the frogs should not decline the snake's request. Similarly, the example of squirrels helping Lord Ram build the bridge to Lanka is used to demonstrate the utility of those who are traditionally considered weak and small. These episodes were inserted to use the Ramayana's popularity to impart moral values consistent with Buddhist principles.[73] As is evident from the priority of his naming in the Laotian epic, Lakshman received particular veneration as a "symbol of brotherly love, loyalty and commitment".[74] Interestingly, Hanuman is the son of Lord Ram's monkey avatar (he turns into a monkey after eating a fruit from an enchanted tree) and Nang Phengsi (the daughter of a sage who too transformed herself into a monkey after the consumption of nikhot – although deliberately). Hanuman assumes a fully human form at the end of the epic.[75] The Phra Lak Phra Ram also mentions Lord Ram founding several cities in what is present-day Thailand, which were governed by his children, such as Muang PhitSanulok, Muang Nakhon Sawan, Muang KrungsriAyutthiya, Muang Khonrat (Nakhon Ratchasima province), and Muang Phimai.

In terms of other diversions from Sanskrit versions, The Phra Lak Phra Ram gives more prominence to the character of Ravan and the pitfalls of pride and arrogance in comparison to the main hero of the epic, Phra Lam. Ravan is said to have moved to Lanka from Cambodia. It is god Indra who blesses Ravan with his mystical powers and his iconography is visible on the walls of Vat Phu in Champasak in the south of Laos.[76] Indra's prominence over Shiva is reminiscent of the Buddhist Tripitaka tales. Sita is born of Ravan and Indra's wife, after the former tricks the latter. However, to exact revenge, Indra's wife is reborn as Ravan's daughter from his wife "Canda". Ravan discards this daughter and she is protected by god Indra until she is adopted by a hermit who names her Sita. Sita grows up and gather acclaim for her beauty, courted by both Lord Ram and Ravan. She is married to Lord Ram, but before he can bring her back to the kingdom of Vientiane (capital city of Laos) she is kidnapped by Ravan and taken to Lanka as a prisoner. After this ensues an epic campaign involving magical beasts, monkey armies, and a bridge across the ocean to Lanka, Ram and his brother invade Ravan's kingdom and Ram kills the demon king Ravan in a duel to free his bride and take her back home to Vientiane.

The Laotian version of the Ramayana also captures an interesting "floating maiden episode," which was first recorded in its highly developed form in a version of the Thai Ramayana or The Ramakien in the late 18th Century. The Thai version is described in great detail by Mary Brockington:

> The 'Floating Maiden' episode occurs when Rāvaṇa learns to his dismay that the vānara army is in the process of building a causeway that will enable them to reach and attack Laṅkā (Rāmakīen 1968, 161–64). The maiden is called Benjakai; she is a rākṣasī, niece of Rāvaṇa, and shares the rākṣasa shape-changing power. As the daughter of Vibhīṣaṇa (Pipek), whose recent defection to Rāma's side has caused Rāvaṇa vindictively to enslave her, her loyalty is divided. She is anxious to see her father again and to escape Rāvaṇa's slavery, but she is also frightened of disobeying her uncle. When Rāvaṇa feigns repentance for banishing Vibhīṣaṇa, and gives her an opportunity to see him again, after a long struggle she agrees to his proposal: to take on Sītā's form and float across to the vāṇara camp, pretending to be dead, in the hope of demoralizing Rāma to the point of giving up the struggle to reclaim Sītā. The ruse initially works, and Rāma is deceived by the illusion, until Hanumān points out that the apparent body does not smell like a corpse and cannot have floated against the tide; he suggests cremating it, at which Benjakai rapidly comes back to life but is captured by Hanumān before she can escape. Rāma soothes Vibhīṣaṇa's anger, and orders Hanumān to take her back to Laṅkā to inform Rāvaṇa that his plan has failed.[77]

In the Thai version, the demoness Benjkai forms a relationship with Hanuman, and they also give birth to a child called Asuraphad, who has the face of a monkey but the body of a demon. She is crucial to the defeat of Ravan, as it is prophesied that Ravan's meditations for mystical powers can only disturbed if his "cave retreat is unblocked by the water in which a rākṣasī has washed her feet". In the Laotian version, this initial story, which itself is a Thai adaptation, the motif is further evolved. The compilation of the Phra Lak Phra Ram by Sachchidanand Sahai in 1996 discusses a telling of the story near Vientiane. Sita's supposed corpse appears to Lord Ram and the army of monkeys on across the ocean from Lanka as a "a transformed banana trunk".[78]

In terms of its cultural imprint, in Laos, "the Ram story [has] featured in many mural paintings and wood relief carvings on temple doors and windows. It was also one of the favourite themes in the repertoire of the Lao Royal Ballet until 1975, and this tradition has been revived since 2002 by the Royal Palace Museum Theatre of Luang Prabang". In fact, the Ramayana is still staged every alternate night at this Theatre. One can also find Palm-leaf manuscripts from different parts of Laos that carry shorter versions of the Phra Lak Phra Ram. One such example is the "Lam Pha Lam", Which is equally popular in Laotian urban centres as well as in rural areas. These shorter versions were created to be sung by a "Mor Lam", a traditional expert singer who is trained to melodically recite lengthy poems and epic literature while being accompanied by a "Khaen" (bamboo mouth organ). Due to Hanuman's popularity and association with ideas of "strength, stamina, agility, intelligence and devotion", his insignia is commonly found on "Yantras" and "protective shirts, headbands, battle standards of entire armies, or, most efficiently and durably, tattooed on a fighter's body".[79] The fabled dance drama based on The Phra Lak Phra Ram of Vientiane is mainly taken from the latter half of the text with the scenes of the tricky separation of Sita, Lord Ram and Lakshman; the kidnapping of Sita by Ravan, the long journey through the forest to the coastline with a dramatic capture of Lanka Island in search for Sita; and the fight, won by the heroes Lord Ram and Lakshman with their army of monkeys. Finally, Lord Ram returns to the city of Vientiane with Sita and Lakshman rules the kingdom".[80]

Chapter 6

Myanmar and The Yama Zatdaw

The Hindu epic Ramayana came to Myanmar with early Indian traders and merchants, some of whom later settled in the country. The oral tradition of the Ramayana in Myanmar is believed to date as far back as the reign of King Anawrahta (1044–77), who is considered the father of the Myanma nation and founder of the first Burmese empire at Bagan. The Ramayana in Myanmar was influenced greatly by the ancient Thai city of Ayutthaya. The Burmese conquest of Ayutthaya in 1767 under the Konbaung dynasty led to the transfer of hundreds of Thai artisans, including palace dancers, musicians, and other performing artists conversant in the tradition of the Ramayana. Such invasions brought back spoils of war, including elements of The Thai Ramakien into Myanmar. "The Yama Zatdaw" is Myanmar's version of the Ramayana, and it is unofficially considered Myanmar's national epic. The story of the Ramayana has become embedded in the culture of Myanmar, and the Myanma people have adapted the stories of the Ramayana to their sensibilities, giving the text a flavour that reflects the local environment and culture of the country. The influence of the Ramayana on Myanmar is evident in the adaptation of its stories, the popularity of the epic, and its integration into various art forms, showcasing a deep cultural impact of this ancient Hindu epic on Myanmar's society. Although the Yama Zatdaw was documented earlier, it continued to be transmitted through oral sources till the 16th century.[81]

Myanmar is predominantly a Theravada Buddhist country, but Hinduism has played a significant role in the region in confluence. For instance, "in the terra-cotta plaques depicting the 550 (or rather 547) Jatakas of the two Hpetleik pagodas, the Rama story is shown as incorporated into the Buddhist tales".[82] Similar to other South East Asian countries, here Lord Ram was considered a predecessor of Lord Buddha, and Burmese term for the Buddhist version of Lord Ram was "Alaung-daw Yama" or the "Bodhisat Rama". His story is mentioned most prominently in the Dasharatha Jataka. It was only sometime after the 16th Century that the Valmiki Ramayana's more enlarged version reached Myanmar via Thailand and other neighbouring countries, and was called the "Pondaw Yama" or the "Nan-dwin Yama". This version became more popular in the Burmese royal courts. Much earlier, there are suggestions that the "early Pyu people" revered Lord Ram as they were Vaisnavites. They were known to be worshippers of Hindu deities and one of their earliest cities was called Beikthano (city of God Vishnu), which existed from about the 1st to 8th Century AD. The city of Taungdwingyi in Myanmar is supposed to have been founded in 837 AD, with the classical name of "Ramavati" (city of Lord Rama). But there are no reliable references to the Ramayana that have been uncovered in this period. The first evidence is found in the "Abeyadana Temple" built during the reign of King Kyansittha

(A.D.1084–1113), which depicts tondoes (circular paintings) of God Vishnu, Lord Ram, and Hanuman. King Kyansittha claimed he was a descendant of God Vishnu and a close relative of Lord Ram in his previous life. This is found in "two of his Mon inscriptions, one from Mya Kan, Bagan the other from the KyaikThalan Pagoda near Thaton.[83]

The first known written Burmese version of the Ramayana was compiled by U Aung Phyo in 1775 titled "Rama Thagyin" (Songs from the Ramayana). U Aung Phyo was known for singing ballads and he probably adapted the Ramayana in poetic form for recitations. There is also a three-volume copy of the Ramayana called "Rama vatthu," which was written on a palm leaf in 1877. Its prose was later extended in the 18th Century as the "Maha Rama (Yama)", and is considered the most complete text of the Ramayana published in Myanmar. The original "parabaik" (folding book) is from around 1870 and has sixteen pages with scenes from the Ramayana painted with brief captions in the local language, and was discovered by the Myanmar Historical Commission around 1972. A copy of the text stored with the US Library of Congress carries the following description:

> The paper covers are painted in red, yellow, and green, with floral borders and prancing lions. One cover has an inscription in black ink in Burmese, giving the title, Rama Zat, and a brief identification of the contents. They are, as follows: Rama strings the bow; Dusakhaya demon in battle; offerings of alms; abduction in the chariot; building of the stone causeway; and arrival in Thiho (Ceylon, or present-day Sri Lanka).[84]

In terms of its performance, the popularity of the Yama Zatdaw in Myanmar reached its zenith during the reign of the famously inept King Bagan (1846–1853) of the Konbaung Dynasty. In 1849, the Ramayana came to be depicted in a continuous series of 347 stone relief sculptures at the pagoda of Maha Loka Marazein of Thakhuttanai. As a side note, the status of such pagodas suffered gradually due to their distance from Myanmar's population centres. Thereafter, Thakin Min Mi, the Chief Queen of Singu Min 1776–1781, as a poet and writer herself, became a strong patron of the Yama Zatdaw. Following her lead, during the reign of King Bodawpaya (1782–1819), performances of the Yama Zatdaw were a staple of the royal courts. He ordered for a committee of members from Myanmar's royal families and aristocracy to produce Burmese translations of the Thai Ramayana. His order read as follows:

> "This is a list of persons responsible for selecting from the completed works such plots and scenes as would be suitable for the Palace and Royal Apartments and responsible for writing in full the poems and songs for the plots and scenes so that they could be sung, presented and acted".

The members of the fabled "Commission of Eight" were:

Writers of Music and Songs

1. Pabhavati, the Lady Thakin Minmi (1758–1798) ex-queen of King Singu (1776–1782). At the time she had remarried the Prince, Lord of Kama town. (He was a son of King Bodawpaya who had succeeded King Singu. This Lord of Kama was the 8th member of this Committee.)
2. Lord of Pyinsitown,the Prince Commander of the Royal Cavalry.

3. U Kyi Soe, Maha Nanda Yodha, Lord of Maletha village and Ngetoe. (He was a Privy Councillor).
4. U Sa (1766–1853), at the time Zeya Thinkhaya, Herald to the Privy Council. (He later became Lord of Myawady, a famous soldier, diplomat, musician and poet).

Writers of Dialogues and Poems

5. Prince Minye Nanda Meit, Lord of Malun town, later Lord of Mekkhara town.
6. Nemyo Kyaw Swa, Assistant Minister, Lord of Moda town.
7. U Toe, author of Rama Yagan; his title was Nemyo Raza-thu, Herald to the Crown Prince and Treasurer.
8. Prince Thado Dhama Raza, Lord of Taungoo town. While he was Lord of Kama town he married Lady Thakin Minmi. The plays completed with plots and scenes were *I-naung, Rama, Sankhapatta, Kesasiri*— 4 plays.[85]

After King Bodawpaya there was a short period of lull, and the Yama Zatdaw was later revived as a theatrical play performed by royal troupes of professional artists under King Tharrawaddy Min (1837–1846) and his son Pagan Min (1847–1853). Under his successor, King Mindon (1853–1878), a first full translation of the "Ramayana Court Drama" was discovered, although the prominence of the Yama Zatdaw remained muted and only special episodes were performed. Notably, Burmese Minister "Myawady Mingyi U Sa converted the Ramayana Jataka into a typical Burmese classical drama, and he also composed theme music and songs for its performance—leading to its adoption as part of stringed puppet shows called "Yama zatpwe" (dramatic performances of the Yama Zatdaw).[86]

Myanmar has a rich literary and art tradition influenced by the Ramayana. In terms of literary texts, it was U Thein Han, a Chief Librarian of the University of Rangoon Library and Chairman of the Burma (Myanmar) Historical Commission, who made the most notable contribution to the study of the Ramayana in Myanmar. According to him, "the earliest literary reference to the Ramayana is in a Myanma pyo (Jataka poem) written by Shin Agga Thamadi in 1527 AD entitled Thuwunna-shan Thahte-khan Pyo, based on the Suvannasama Jataka. There are also two references to the Ramayana from the first half of the 18th century in the Exegesis by the Min Kyaung Sayadaw".[87] The Hindu epic has also inspired romantic poems, which became popular among Myanmar's royalty. Scenes from the Hindu epic are still depicted in murals, paintings, and sculptures in temples and pagodas across the country. Such scenes can also be found as motifs or design elements in Burmese lacquerware and wood carvings. The characters of Lord Ram, Sita, Hanuman, and other key figures are commonly represented in religious art. Depictions of the Ramayana are also part of the famous Burmese pictorial textile art known as "*kalaga*", which underwent a major revival in the final decades of the Konbaung dynasty. These art forms usually present "selected highlights that focus on the most beloved moments in the narrative".[88] Stone sculptures of Lord Ram and Hanuman can also be found in the Nathlaung Temple (dedicated to god Vishnu) in Bagan.

The Ramayana has also been adapted into various forms of performing arts in Myanmar, such as dance-drama and puppet shows. It is so popular that the Myanma city of Pyapon hosted a one-day closed-door performance at the Shwe Nat Gu Pagoda even during the Covid-19 pandemic. The Thai version of the Ramayana, which includes masked dance performances, has been influential in Myanmar's theatrical, musical, and artistic traditions as well. However, unlike in Thailand where performers do not speak, the Myanma actors lift up their masks to articulate dialogues. It is notable that dramatic performances based on the Ramayana were incredibly popular amongst Myanmar's aristocracy. The following is a first-hand account of British Envoy Michael Symes on 10th April 1795, who saw such a performance at the residence of the Governor of the HanthawadiMon provincial region, which then included Yangon:

> At a little before eight o' clock, the hour when the play was to commence, we proceeded to the house of the Maywoon, accompanied by Baba-Sheen, who, on all occasions, acted as master of the ceremonies. The theatre was the open court, splendidly illuminated by lamps and torches; the Maywoon and his lady sat in a projecting balcony of his house; we occupied seats below him, raised about two feet from the ground and covered with carpets; a crowd of spectators were seated in a circle round the stage. The performance began immediately on our arrival, and far excelled any Indian drama I had ever seen. The dialogue was spirited, without rant, and the action animated, without being extravagant: the dresses of the principal performers were showy and becoming. I was told that the best actors were natives of Siam, a nation which, though unable to contend with the Birmans and Peguers in war, have cultivated with more success the refined arts of peace. By way of an interlude between the acts, a clownish buffoon entertained the audience with a

recital of different passages, and by grimace, and frequent alterations of tone and countenance, extorted loud peals of laughter from the spectators. The Birmans seem to delight in mimicry, and are very expert in the practice, possessing uncommon versatility of countenance.[89]

The relationship of this performance with the Ramayana is expounded in greater detail by Dr. Francis Buchanan, who accompanied the British Envoy on his mission to Myanmar:

> Although these entertainments, like the Italian opera, consists of music, dancing, action, with a dialogue in recitative, yet we understood, that no part but the songs was previously composed. The subject [of the play] is generally taken from some of the legends of their heroes, especially of Rama; and the several parts, songs and actions, being assigned to different performers, the recitative part or dialogue is left to each actors' ingenuity. If, from the effects on the audience, we might judge of the merit of the performance, it must be very considerable, as some of the performers had the art of keeping the multitude in a roar. I often, however, suspected, that the audience, were not difficult to please; for I frequently observed the Myoowun of Haynthawade [Hamsavati or Hanthawadi] (the man of high rank whom we most frequently saw, thrown into immoderate laughter by the most childish contrivances.) The [Ramayana] and other ancient fabulous histories, form the groundwork of nearly all the favourite plays, the outline of the story being merely preserved, while the language of the play depends as much upon the fancy of the performer as the taste of the audience.[90]

James George Scott (1851–1935), a colonial officer who served in Myanmar after its annexation by the British also had similar views:

> Everything was of the best possible kind; the royal drum and cymbal harmonicons, the trumpets, the flutes, even

> the bamboo clappers, were of an excellence never before known in Rangoon. The players were famous wherever Burmese was spoken, and the play lasted five nights. The general opinion was that it called forth more admiration of King Mindon than loyalty for the Empress [Victoria] among the delta people.[91]

It is abundantly clear from these commentaries that the Ramayana was a source of great influence on the cultural milieu of pre-modern Myanmar, and was celebrated and performed with grace and colour, and enjoyed increasing prominence in Myanmar's royal courts. For instance, when the "Mandalay Palace was constructed in 1857, there was a temporary Royal Theatre building near the Hman Nan Saung (the Central Palace)". However, in 1885, when the last Burmese ruler, King Thibaw was sent into exile by the British from upper Myanmar, "the Ramayana Court Dramatic Troupe" was disbanded.[92] But colonial officials continued to patronise performances of the Ramayana during special occasions as part of their attempts to legitimise their governance. After Myanmar's independence in 1948, the Ministry of Culture has encouraged the Ramayana as a cultural performance. The most complete adaption of the Ramayana in Myanmar for drama—written in both poetry and prose—remains the undated "Thiri Yama" authored by Nemyo Nataka Kyaw Gaung.

Chapter 7

Philippines and The Maharadia Lawana

> The presence of numerous words with Sanskrit root in Tagalog (Filipino language); the Laguna Copper Plate inscription – the oldest artefact discovered in the Philippines written in Kavi derived from Pallava script; the golden statue of Agusan Tara; and the local version of Indian epic Ramayana called the 'Maharadia Lawana', testify to the historical cultural linkages that existed between India and the Philippines.
>
> —Official Website of the Indian Embassy in Manila[93]

In the Philippines, the Ramayana has been adapted in the form of the Maharadia Lawana, which is an ancient Filipino epic, often considered one of the most important and oldest pre-colonial literary works in the Philippines. This epic is part of the Maranao literary tradition and is believed to have originated from the Maranao people of Mindanao, who are a predominantly Muslim Filipino ethnic group residing in an island in the southern Philippines. The Maharadia Lawana narrates the adventures and exploits of the legendary monkey-king "Lawana". The text is a prose tale in Maranaw, the language of the Maranao people, and is considered their national epic. It is believed to have arrived in the Philippines between the 17th to 19th Century due to the intensity of maritime trade and migration between South East Asia and the Indian subcontinent across the Bay of Bengal. The story of the Ramayana reached the Philippines via Javanese and Malay continuous language versions and has successively been passed down as the Maharadia Lawana through oral tradition. Its English translation is credited to Filipino Indologist Juan R. Francisco and was proof read by his teacher the Maranao scholar NagasuraMadale. Francisco carried out ethnographic research in the Lake Lanao area in the summer of 1968 and discovered the text in a madrassa.[94] It was shown to him by Dr.Mamitua Saber of the Mindanao State University, "who had taken it from the region of Bai Pamoki of Taraka, Lanao del Sur.[95] The text is a significant cultural and literary work that reflects the unique cultural perspectives and orientations of the Maranao people. It is a local adaptation of the Ramayana from other South East Asian countries, indigenised to suit the cultural perspectives, and orientations of the Maranao peoples.

The most notable feature of the epic is that it is told from the perspective of the antagonist Ravan or Maharadia Lawana. Ravan is said to be the descendant of the great Sultan and Sultana of Pulu Bandiarmasir (Lanka) and is born with 7/8 heads. He is exiled to Pulu Nagara by his father due to his intemperate misdeeds and complaints from the local population. This is when Ravan becomes an ascetic and practices penance and prays to Allah to achieve spiritual enlightenment and mastery over mystical powers. When Ravan tries to self-immolate, he receives a blessing of immortality from the angel "Diabarail". He then returns to his kingdom as a new avatar. In another kingdom called

Agama Niog (Ayodhya), Lord Ram or "Radia Mangandiri" and Lakshman or "Radia Mangawarna" are born to the Sultan and Sultaness. The brothers subsequently embark upon a ten-year journey to the Sultanate of Pulu Nabandai, to seek courtship with the Sultan's daughter "TuwanPotre Malaila Tihaia" or Sita. In the course of their voyage, the encounter tempestuous waves and are shipwrecked on the shores of Pulu Nabandai. They are eventually nursed back to their full strength by an elderly local woman named Kabayan. Thereafter, Lord Ram succeeds in winning over Sita's hand in a game of *"Sipa"* (Philippines' traditional native sport played with a Rattan ball), and later is also required to slay a giant snake to fulfil a vow of the Bai of Pulu Nabandai (Sita's mother). Subsequently, the married couple begin to plot their journey homewards. On one fateful day however, Ravan, disguised as a deer with golden horns entices Sita. She demands the deer's capture and Lord Ram undertakes to do the same. However, the deer is an illusion and he is unsuccessful. Lakshman too is compelled to follow Lord Ram's footsteps in search of the dear when he hears a 'cry for help' in his brother's voice. However, this is a charade. When the brothers return to their shelter they find out that Ravan has abducted Sita.

It is at this juncture, as Lord Ram and Lakshman are faced with the despondency of Sita's abduction that "Lakshmana" or Hanuman is introduced in the story. He is a born in monkey form of a chance encounter between Lord Ram and the Queen of the East, PotreLangawi in a dream sequence, as the former's body falls into and drifts through subconsciously along a river. Hanuman raises an army of water buffaloes and monkeys to help Lord Ram and Lakshman's quest to retrieve Sita from Ravan. It is mentioned that every time whenever Ravan approaches Sita, a fire barrier appears between them. Instead of Sita having to walk through fire at the end of the Hindu epic as a "test of purity", fire as an element is seen protecting Sita's purity during her abduction itself. After locating Sita, Lord Ram, Lakshman, and Hanuman have to build and cross a bridge woven of vines to reach Ravan's Sultanate. When crocodiles attack the bridge, Hanuman defeats them. They swear their allegiance to Lord Ram thereafter. Eventually, Lord Ram confronts Ravan in combat and strikes a debilitating blow with a sword honed upon a fabled whetstone set upon Naga wood in the heart of Lanka— a weapon prophesied as the sole means to subdue Ravan's might. Ravan's death is shrouded in some mystery at the end of this Filipino epic, and there no mention of Sita's test of loyalty or her children. The story ends with Hanuman shedding his Monkey avatar and transforming into a human, and the heroes making their journey back to Lord Ram's Sultanate in Agama Niog riding on the backs of crocodiles. Moreover, the Maharadia Lawana is extremely brief and details of birth of various characters, the reason why Ravan abducted Sita and other key episodes are missing.[96]

Interestingly, despite originating from the Maranao peoples, the text only has faint influences of Islam, unlike the Malaysian Hikayat Seri Rama, which links the provenance of key characters to Allah. Filipino Indologist Juan R. Francisco describes this as follows:

> In the long years of encounter between Islam and the indigenous cultures as well as the culture that was introduced by Spaniards and the Americans in the later

> years of Philippine history, conflicts were inevitable. But in the process certain adjustments had to be made by each to be able to coexist peacefully later on. These adjustments, one of which is seen in the development of the song or hymn as part of the Islamic literature in the Philippines, are important and meaningful. For the indigenous and the alien—Islam and Christianity—shall be in constant contact in the years to come. The alien had come to stay, and yet it has to draw its nourishment from the soul and the soil of the indigenous.[97]

In Francisco's reading, the prior existence of indigenous knowledge of Hindu epics meant that later Islamic dominance had to accommodate and co-exist with these forms of influence. This was also aided by the fact that the contact of Islam in these parts was not so direct, and there were hardly any Islamic missionaries having direct knowledge of key texts such as the Koran, causing an Islamic overlay on Maranaw culture. This symbiosis came under strain as pilgrimages to Islamic centres of devotion in the Arab world picked up steam. But Maranao system of religious belief were still retained, despite in some cases being non-Islamic (cgs. belief in river gods and the worship of the dead by setting aside food for the spirit of the newly dead and periodic revisits). One such Filipino practice that forced the sanction of Islam was "the practice of the kalilang", which was a feast which involving the calling of water spirits, "tonong", to protect the new born or to bring health to the ill. Another custom of obvious pagan origin was the inclusion of "spirit houses" in the eaves of dwellings and in the fields. Therefore, despite this "encounter between an indigenous culture and an intrusive one, Islam, showed certain of the accommodations made by both to make the society viable in not only the religious, but also all other aspects of Maranaw culture".[98] This capacity for perseverance would later be tested by the invasion of Christian Spanish and American cultures in the Philippines.

The Ramayana has left its mark on Filipino arts and moral values, and dramatic performances. The famous Filipino "Singkil" dance, rooted in the Ramayana, is a cherished folk dance of the Maranao people of Lake Lanao. The Singkil dance is often performed during festive occasions and cultural events in the Philippines. It tells the story of the "Darangan," an epic poem of the Maranao people of Mindanao, which has influences from Hindu epics like the Ramayana. The dance narrates the tale of Princess Gandingan who, like Sita in the Ramayana, is portrayed as a woman of grace and virtue. One of the most iconic elements of the Singkil dance is the use of bamboo poles, which are skilfully manipulated and clapped together by the dancers. The intricate footwork, including weaving through the moving bamboo poles, is said to symbolize the princess's agile movements as she navigates through various challenges. This part of the dance is often referred to as the "tinkling" or bamboo dance, and it is not directly from the Ramayana but is a distinctive Filipino addition to the Singkil performance. The dance form is described in great detail by the scholar Joefe B. Santarita in his study of India–Philippines cultural relations:

> Singkil, for instance, is an elegant, stylized performance dance usually involving performers interpreting archetype characters inspired by and interpreted from the thread of storylines found similarly in the Indian epic Ramayana—including a princess, her faithful assistant, friends, as well

> as ardent suitors who would be stepping in and out, sitting or standing on two sets of bamboo poles crossed, and being thumped on the floor and hit together by men to make percussive music for the dance. Native music instruments like the agung (gong) and the kulintang (made of eight small gongs set on a rack) complete the ensemble of musical instruments in the dance. The Maranaw people in southern Philippines even before the arrival of the Spaniards in 16th century and the arrival of the Islam religion in the Philippines by the 12th century observed these oral traditions by re-telling similar storiesfound in the Indian epic Ramayana into 'Darangen'. This re-telling is the basis of the story being interpreted and performed, whenever the Singkil is danced.
>
> The body, arms, and hand swaying and movements in this dance remind ancient dance forms from many countries of the Hindu-style of dancing, which in the Singkil can be explained by the extensive influences made by the Sri-Vijaya and Majapahit empires that reached Indonesia as well as the many islands of the Philippines. In the performance, the main dancer—Princess Gandingan—interprets the movements after learning the rituals from her mother, the powerful healer in the village, in gathering medicinal plants and herbs from the forest. Movements that interpret Gandingan's sojourn in the forest, either alone or with her friends and faithful assistant that usually bear a beautiful parasol for the princess wherever she goes during the dance.[99]

The story of Maharadia Lawana is a testament to the enduring influence of Indian culture and the Ramayana in the Philippines, particularly among the Maranao people. It exemplifies the process of cultural indigenization, where foreign narratives are adapted and transformed to reflect the local cultural context and values. The Maharadia Lawana is a significant literary work that has contributed to the preservation and promotion of Maranao cultural heritage and identity. The text has simultaneously become an integral part of the social fabric of the Maranao people, and its characters and episodes are integrated into various forms of traditional performing arts, such as classical dance-dramas, and also artwork, weaving, wood, plastic and metal crafts.

Chapter 8

The Ramayana in China and Tibet

> The Ramayana is an "eternal fountain of the Indian literary creation", and "not only [a] valuable collection of the great literature of the Indian people, but also [a] priceless treasure of the world".
>
> —Chinese scholars Yu Longyu and Meng Zhaoyi[100]

Like other South East Asian countries, Buddhist influences played a key role in the transmission of the Ramayana to China and Tibet. The Ramayana, being a significant part of Indian cultural and religious heritage, was introduced to China and Tibet through Buddhist monks and scholars who frequently migrated between these states. Chinese and Khotanese versions of the Ramayana have been recited in Jataka form, and are popular in the Tai-speaking Dai ethnic area of China, in the Yunnan province. The Hindu epic is believed to have been transmitted to China across the Sichuan-Yunnan-Burma-India route. On the other hand, Tibet had differing experience of how the Ramayana came to its lands and was popularly disseminated as an epic. The Tibetan version of the Ramayana, found in incomplete manuscript form in the Dunhuang Caves, is written in an early Tibetan language. Some scholars argue that "it belongs to the earlier genre of "royal" Ramayanas, popular with kings of South and Southeast Asia, unlike the later *"bhakti"* Ramayanas".[101]

One of the most vivid references to the Ramayana in China is found at the Kaiyuan Temple in Quanzhou, which carries Hindu influence from the 11th and 13th century. Japanese scholar Nakano Miyoko in his essay titled "Fujian Province and the Journey to the West[102]," has offered the following interpretation of the Kaiyuan Temple:

> At the Kaiyuan Temple in Quanzhou, there was a pagoda built in the first year (1237 AD) of the Jiaxi Period during the Southern Song Dynasty. On the wall of the fourth floor of the West Pagoda, there was a relief of a monkey wearing a golden ring with a string of beads around the neck. On his vest hung a roll of Buddhist scripture. On his right shoulder there was a tiny image of a monk. It is not certain whether the image was that of Xuanzang. On the other walls on the same floor of this pagoda, there were images of Xuanzang. Furthermore, in a Brahmanist temple in Quanzhou, on a huge pillar was a relief of a monkey whose tail was very long and in whose hand there was something like grass. This naturally reminds us of Hanuman in the Ramayana who, with his tail on fire, once burnt down Lanka. This monkey also carried a mountain with a magic herb on his hand to save the lives of Rama and Laksmana.

It is notable that outside India, the Chinese Buddhist work "Mahavibhasa", a well-known commentary on the Jnanaprasthana of Katyayaniputra, is considered to be the oldest record of the Ramayana outside of India. According to fable Chinese traveller Hsuan-Tsang, this text was originally written between 120–162 AD during the reign of King Kanishka.[103] However, this was refuted by T. Walters, as the text makes a reference to a previous incident during Kanishka's regime. A positive conclusion has remained elusive for scholars although K. Watanabe traces it to somewhere prior to the 4th Century.[104] More specific parts of the Hindu epic are said to have travelled eastwards along with other Jataka stories such as King Dasharatha, Anamaka Jataka, and Shambuka. In the Anamaka Jataka, Lord Ram is a previous birth of Lord Buddha or a Bodhisattva. His enemy is not Ravan, but his uncle who usurps the throne. In Buddhist fashion, Lord Ram resigns to the forest, where his wife is abducted by a "naga" or serpent. Aligning with the monkey army, Lord Ram kills the serpent and rescues Sita.

Chinese scholar Jin Kemu has examined the "Collection of Writings About the Six Paramitas, Volume 5", translated during the Three Kingdoms (Wu state, 3rd century AD). He finds that the text tells the story of "the Monkey King" (presumed to be Hanuman) and also mentions the Shambuka Jataka, in which King Dasharatha punishes Lord Ram with exile for killing a shudra ascetic, Shambuka. In terms of other Chinese texts, as B.R. Deepak notes, the "Buddhacarita" translated during the Northern Liang (5th century), and "Mahavibhasa Sutra" (volume 46) translated by Xuanzang during the Tang Dynasty (7th century) also have references to the Ramayana. Xuanzang's The Great Tang Dynasty Record of the Western Regions too references stories from the Ramayana in its portrayal of the Kingdom of Peshawar and Kingdom of Pushkarvati. The Chinese translation of the "Lankavatara Sutra" and the ancient

Buddhist text "Saṃyukta Ratna Piṭaka Sutra" mention the Ramayana as well. Professor Deepak argues that "these texts were prevalent mostly among various polities of the present-day Xinjiang and highly defragmented polities ruled by the Han Chinese".[105] The Chinese Ramayanas rename the key characters from the Hindu epic as Lomo (Lord Ram), Poloto (Bharat), Loman (Lakshman), Tsau Lamma (King Dasharatha), and Nangsida (Sita). Across different versions, Ravan is described as an evil "Naga" king.

A striking similarity also exists between Chinese references to The Monkey King "Sun Wukong" in the fabled Chinese novel "Journey to the West" published during the Ming Dynasty (16th Century) and Hanuman. Initially, it was believed that Sun Wukong had evolved from the image of a water goblin (Huai river monster, Wu Zhiqi) in Chinese mythology. For instance, Chinese scholar Lu Xun in his collection on a "Brief History of Chinese Fiction" has argued that: "Since the Song and Yuan dynasties, the saying has been widely circulated amongst the people and scholars… it was not until the Ming vintage Journey to the West by Wu Cheng'en that this supernatural image was transformed into a fast-moving figure in the form of Sun Wukong, as a result, the water goblin mythology was completely buried". However, soon thereafter, in 1923, Chinese scholar Hu Shi refuted Lu Xun's point of view and said: "I have always suspected that this magical monkey is not a domestic product, but an Indian import. Perhaps even the myth Wu Zhiqi is also created and influenced by India…. Therefore, I rely on the guidance of Dr.Baror A. von Staël Holstein who argues that in Ramayana there is a Hanuman, which is probably the real image of the monkey king, Sun Wukong".

B.R. Deepak highlights a third theory of Sun Wukong's origins as well, which is supported by scholars such as Cai Guoliang and Xiao Bing. This "Hybrid theory" argues that the image of Sun Wukong cannot exclude the local as well as foreign influence. As per noted Chinese scholar Ji Xianlin, who I will discuss in some detail later: "We can't refute the relationship between Sun Wukong and Nala and Hanuman of the Ramayana. However, at the same time, it cannot be denied that Chinese authors have further developed Sun Wukong, and have innovatively, combined the Indian monkeys with China's Wu Zhiqi. With their powerful imagination and refinement, they have created the brave and bold, lively and artistic image of Sun Wukong, which is loved by the people".[106] While the exact proportion of Hanuman's influence on the characterisation of Sun Wukong is unclear, it is amply evident that Indian literary influences and the Ramayana did play a prominent role considering the geographical conditions and the history of cultural transmission between India and China.

It is believed that the Dai nationality of China was the first to assimilate Ramayana (Lang ka sip ho and Ta Lamma versions in Dai) in its folk tradition as part of the import of Buddhism. The "Dai" are a cross-border ethnic group in Yunnan, China, and are unique because of their geographical location closer to the Vietnamese border, allowing Indo-Buddhist influences to permeate via South East Asia. Feng Hanyong argues that one of the gateways for the Ramayana to reach the Dai peoples was via the Sichuan-Tibet Highway, and was opened no later than the 4th century BC. The Ramayana has greatly influenced the literary traditions of this region, for instance in the production of the epic poem Lan Ga Xi He of the Dai nationality. Chinese scholar Yuyun Xue has examined such influences in detail. He highlights that "Lan Ga Xi He", who is known amongst the Dai peoples as one of the "five sage poets", and the text Twelve-head Devil were both influenced by the Ramayana.

As per Wang Song and his book "A Preliminary Study on the Development of Dai Poetry," Buddhist scriptures carrying Indian undercurrents had found roots in the Dai region around the 1st Century AD, they only became popular around 8th century AD. Thereafter, "From the 14th to 15th centuries AD, the [Ramayana] was [adopted] by the Dai poet Ying Da Wan into the Lan Ga Xi He with more than 12,000 lines". These versions of the Ramayana also came to be expressed with Dai characteristics. This was done by "adding the ancient legend of the Dai people, and replacing the name of the hero in the original story with the name of their hero in Mengzhai. The 'Large and Small Lan Ga' people referred to, except for the story structure and main characters of Ramayana, are all Dai ethnicized. Later, the Dai language came into being, and the long-term oral chanting Ramayana was adapted into Lan Ga Xi He and Twelve-head Devil in the time of Payazhen. In Lan Ga Xi He, the various ancient Indian characteristics carried in Ramayana have been transformed into the characteristics of the Dai ethnic group. The religious aspect is particularly obvious, that is, the background of the story has changed from Hinduism to Southern Buddhism".[107]

The most notable modern Chinese version of the Ramayana in China comes from the Chinese scholar Ji Xianlin, who founded the Department of Eastern Languages at Peking University, and became the first Chinese to translate Ramayana from Sanskrit into Chinese. It took him almost a decade to render this epic in Chinese with 200,000 odes and nearly 90,000 lines in 8 volumes published in 1984. His achievement is made more gargantuan by the fact that he did so at the apogee of Mao's Cultural Revolution, at great risk to his life and well-being. Recognising Professor Ji's contribution to Indology, the Government of India awarded him Padma Bhushan award in 2008. In 2012, it was reported that his translated version of the Ramayana would be displayed at a library in a culture park in Kailash Mansarovar by the India–China Economic and Cultural Council.[108] Scholars such as Ji Xianlin were an artefact of a period of cultural renaissance in post-Cultural Revolution China under Deng Xiaoping and his policies of cultural autonomy instead of assimilation.

The Tibetan Ramayana on the other hand, does not allude to the Buddhist Ramayana and also has many plots at variance with The Valmiki Ramayana. It is compiled of verses, reflecting spoken conversations and discourses between Lord Ram and Sita. The story is recounted in prose, and it does not lose its Indian roots, but changes itself to adopt the culture of Tibet to sustain as a parallel literature. The Tibetan Ramayana is a significant cultural and literary work that reflects the unique cultural perspectives and orientations of the Tibetan people. It is a local adaptation of the Ramayana, indigenized to suit Tibetan cultural perspectives and orientations. The Tibetan Ramayana has been a subject of scholarly study across a millennium and is considered an important part of the cultural heritage of Tibet. Both, the Chinese and Tibetan texts are part of a broader tradition in this region, which also comprises Tocharian, Khotanese, and Uighur manuscripts and manuscript fragments from Central Asia, and later adaptations in Mongolian.

The Tibetan Ramayana, unlike the Chinese version which is in Jataka form in prose, is compiled in verse form (around 250). Even before the time of the manuscript versions found in the Magao caves in Dunhuang (Eastern Xinjiang), the Ramayana story was circulating in Tibet for centuries in Oral Tradition. Bengali Buddhist monk Prajñāvarman, has briefly discussed episodes from the Ramayana related to King Dasharatha and his sons and the abduction of Sita, in his two stotra commentaries, which were translated to Tibetan around the 11th Century.[109] The most famous manuscripts of the Ramayana however, are the ones found in Dunhuang. They were discovered in the early twentieth century, by British explorers Sir Aurel Stein and Paul Pelliot, as part of a larger discovery of manuscripts in the various languages of the Silk Road. Among them were these seven Tibetan manuscript fragments of the Ramayana, which are now kept in the British Library (previously India Office Library) and the Bibliothèque Nationale.

In 1929, In 1929 F. W. Thomas identified these manuscripts as containing stories from the Ramayana.[110] They are believed to have been written somewhere between the 8th and 11th Century, mostly in verse form which was typical of Tibetan bardic literature. The text is accessible in English through the efforts of Jan Willem de Jong, who edited and translated the manuscripts.[111] The geographical setting of the epic is predictably Himalayan, evidenced in the description of Lanka which is believed to be situated on Mount Sumeru (known only from Buddhist cosmology). There are also some notable Khotanese influences from

Central Asia. For instance, Lord Ram asks Sugriva to fix a mirror on his body so that he may be easily identified in his duel with Bali. This anecdote is not present in any of the Indian versions of the Ramayana.[112]

There are several notable departures from The Valmiki Ramayana. Lord Ram was not distinguished as a king or as the embodiment of Lord Buddha or God Vishnu. Sita or Rol-rñed-ma is a daughter of Dasgriva or Ravan, who after being discarded due to a portentous prophecy is found in a furrow and raised by two peasants. She is later offered to Lord Ram as wife and he gives her the name Sita. Lakshman rules Ayodhya in Lord Ram's absence and not Bharat. To abduct Sita, Ravan takes the shape of an Elephant and later a Horse, instead of an ascetic asking for alms. After Sita refuses to mount Ravan in either animal form, he cannot touch her without her consent due to fear of bursting into flames. So, he lifts the entire chunk of ground on which she stands and flies away. Three monkeys—Pagsu, Sindu, Hanumanta—thereafter go in search of Sita. There is significant emphasis on letter writing as a medium of communication. Upon finding her in Lanka, along with Lord Ram's ring, the three monkeys give Sita his letter as well. Sita too pens her reply. Other variances in the Tibetan version are succinctly stated by Devdutt Pattanaik:[113]

> King Dasharatha worships Arhats (Buddhist sages?) and is given a flower by the gods, which his chief queen shares with the junior queen. The junior queen delivers a son, Ram, a few days before the senior queen delivers Lakshman. The king dies unable to decide who should be king. Ram, the elder son of the junior queen, is chosen but he abdicates for Lakshman, who in turn, places Ram's footwear on the throne, and chooses to be minister. We do

> not hear about Bharat and Shatrughna here, nor anything about the forest exile.
>
> Sita here is the daughter of Ravan (as in Jain Ramayana). Advised by oracles, he puts her in a copper box, throws her into the sea. The baby makes her way to a water channel being dug by a farmer. She eventually marries Ram. Ram and Sita's separation happens not only because of Ravan's sister named Phurpala here, who is upset at being rejected by Ram, but also because Sita wrongly accuses Lakshman of vile thoughts so that he goes to Ram's rescue, while he is out hunting Ravan's demon-deer.
>
> While looking for Sita, Ram encounters a black river which is blood flowing from Sugirva's eyes, ears and nose after he has been beaten by his elder brother Bali. Sugriva ties a mirror to his tail, challenges Bali to a duel and gets Ram to kill his violent elder brother, promising to find Sita in exchange. During the search for Sita, Hanuman encounters Swayamprahha in a cave and the wingless Sampati on the sea-shore (as in Valmiki Ramayana).
>
> During the war, Ravan becomes invisible. Ram challenges him to show at least one part of his body in keeping Kshatriya dharma. Ravan then reveals only his right toe. Looking at the right toe Ram is able to figure out where his ten heads are located and shoots the arrow at the right head to kill him. The first of Ravan's ten heads is that of a horse/donkey (as in Pahari miniature paintings), which is where his life is located.
>
> In the Tibetan Ramayana, Ram doubts the chastity of Sita and sends her out of the palace. Hanuman argues his case of Sita's innocence successfully and Rama and Sita are united and they stay together happily.

The end of the Tibetan Ramayana is a happier one compared to the Valmiki Ramayana. However, Sita's prominence is diminished. As Ulrike Roesler argues,

> the Dunhuang version [has]… [a] limited emphasis on female characters and issues. Sītā certainly experiences dramatic moments; however, there is only a very moderate portrayal of her emotional trials and tribulations. She seems remarkably pragmatic and even puts up with her exile in the forest without much complaint. When she is invited back to the palace for the big happy ending, there is no trace of a conflict. Compared to the detailed description of Rāvaṇa's story at the beginning and the scenes of battle and friendship between humans and monkeys, the fate of the heroine is relatively marginal. She is extremely beautiful, a bit hasty in her judgment and follows her desire rather than proper deliberation, but she is not portrayed as a negative character; this is more or less all we can deduce.

Roesler finds that instead of the relationship between Lord Ram and Sita getting prominence, Sita's depiction is reduced to aesthetic value and it is instead the heroism and warrior ethics of the key protagonists that are emphasised, along with a shrewd display of the struggle for power and the importance of kingship. Clan structures and Hanuman's allegiance and loyalty to Lord Ram draw praise. This corelated with the motifs of Tibetan society as "in ancient Tibet, the heads of the aristocracy and the king swore a mutual oath of loyalty and support every year, and rituals of confirming mutual loyalty have continued even into more recent times".[114] It becomes clear thus that in Tibet and China too, the Ramayana was used as a political tool of legitimacy. As B.R. Deepak argues "The Hans used it to propagate Buddhism, and often emphasized morality, loyalty and filial piety. The Dai used it to praise the feudal lord system and to sing praises of Buddhism. Tibetans used the Golden Age of Rama to praise local governors". This is somewhat intrinsic to nature of the Ramayana as an epic. Scholars such as Richman have found that the Ramayana is "inherently political since it sets forth normative ideals for kinship, rank and status, and a utopian society".[115]

However, one key difference in the Tibetan and Chinese versions is that due to its lack of Buddhist influence, the former does not expend effort to impart moral values or teachings. However, in Tibet, the Ramayana also became a tool to usher national consciousness. The litterateur Döndrup Gyel is credited with writing such a free verse version of the Hindu epic, counter-intuitively, "to release Tibetan literature from its alleged cultural colonizer, India" after the end of the Cultural Revolution.[116]Gyel questions India's prominence with respect to the Ramayana, arguing that it had transcended its Sanskrit origins:

> The Story of Rāmaṇa not only attained great value and status in the history of the development of Indian literary arts, it also attained great value and status in the history of the development of world literary arts… it spread around the world so that most national literature is influenced by it. For that reason, the Story of Rāmaṇa is a famous work of the literary arts of each people of the world. It is a precious intellectual treasure of each nationality of the world.
>
> Now, if one asks whether there was a version of the Story of Rāmaṇa in our snowy homeland of Tibet, there was… in the trove [of manuscripts] found from Dunhuang, four fragments of the Story of Rāmaṇa emerged… After that, there were a great many writings by former Tibetan scholars which were versions of the Story of Rāmaṇa, either in verse or prose… [these] renditions, commentaries, and poetic exemplars like the stars of the sky are too innumerable to count.

Subsequently, there were many Tibetan commentaries on the Ramayana, for instance by Sakya Pandit Kunga Rgyal-Mtshan and his disciple Dmar-stonChos-kyirgyal-po. Both their versions incorporate greater influences from The Valmiki Ramayana. For the purposes of dramatic performances, the best-known Tibetan adaptation is written by Chöwang Drakpa, who wrote "The Song of Gandharva Maiden's Lute" and "Tale of Ramana". According to other scholars, this text was a "formidable literary challenge, both to read and emulate" and became "a much sought-after style of composition among Tibetan intellectuals...as it was beyond the grasp of common people and gave an elitist touch". There are more modern Tibetan commentaries by Ju Mipam Gyatso as well.[117] Furthermore, "in addition to these independent versions, episodes of the Rāma story have also been preserved in Tibetan commentaries on Daṇḍin's Kāvyādarśa, which became very influential in Tibet from the thirteenth century onwards, and in commentaries on didactic poetry".[118] However, the literary history of the Tibetan Ramayana between the production of the Dunhuang manuscripts and the mid-thirteenth century remains a mystery.

Chapter 9

Japan's Hobutsushu and Sambo-ekotoba

The cultural influence of India on Japan is a fascinating aspect of the historical and cultural interactions between these two countries. While the direct historical connections between India and Japan are limited, the cultural diffusion between the two nations has been significant. The most profound and enduring cultural influence from India to Japan is Buddhism. Buddhism originated in India and spread to various parts of Asia, including Japan. The introduction of Buddhism to Japan is traditionally attributed to Prince Shotoku in the 6th Century. Japanese monks and scholars travelled to India to study Buddhism and bring back scriptures. The fusion of Buddhist ideas with existing Shinto beliefs played a crucial role in shaping Japanese culture, art, and philosophy. Buddhist art and architecture, characterized by intricate carvings, statues, and pagodas, have left a lasting impact on Japanese art. The design of Japanese temples and pagodas often reflects elements of Indian Buddhist architecture, such as the lotus flower and the Bodhi tree. The Ramayana too, is part of this larger transmission of cultural ideas from India to Japan, as Buddhist scriptures and texts introduced Sanskrit and Pali philosophical concepts into the

Japanese language. For example, in Japan, there are seven traditional deities known as the Seven Gods of Fortune. Three of these have a Hindu provenance: Daikokuten is the god of commerce and prosperity (a direct translation of the Sanskrit name Mahākāla which is the Buddhist name for god Shiva); Bishamonten is the god of fortune in war and battles (similar to god Kubera and is also known by the name Vaisravana); and Benzaiten or the goddess of financial fortune, talent, beauty and music (modelled after goddess Sarasvati).[119]

In pre-modern Japan, the Ramayana came to be known as Ramaenna or Ramaensho. In these versions, the character of Hanuman was notably missing. In the "Suwaengi no koto," which is a Japanese adaption of the Ramayana written in the fourteenth century, "Koga Saburo Yorikata, is the youngest son whose exile is caused by his brothers". In another version called "Bontenkoku, Tamawaka (Lord Ram) is a flute player who escapes with his abducted wife Himegini (Sita) while her captor King Baramon (Ravan) is away for hunting". There are also other lesser known Japanese adaptations such as Kifune no honji, Onzoshishimawatari and Bukkigun. These texts have explored deeper convergences between the characters of Lord Ram and Ravan.[120] Buddhism came to Japan via China, carrying Hindu influences. Thus, it is hardly surprising to note that versions of the Ramayana made their way in time from China to Japan. Despite the absence of direct contact, Indian influence was so prominent in Japan that Fabio Rambelli argues that "until the nineteenth century, the Japanese Buddhists envisioned a world system in which India (Tenjiku) was the centre, china was located at the periphery and Japan was an even more isolated territorial entity". India appeared as "a largely imaginary realm in Japanese cultural representations".[121]

The most comprehensive work on the Japanese Ramayana is done by The Japanese Sanskrit scholar Minoru Hara. Robert P. Goldman and Sally J. Sutherland Goldman describe her work as follows:

> Minoru Hara has studied two interesting texts derived from Chinese Buddhist sources. The first is an abridgement of the Rama legend found in the twelfth-century collection of popular tales, the Hobutsushu of TairanoYasuyori that appears to derive from a Chinese canonical Liu-po-lo-mi-ching (otherwise known as Liu-tu-tsi-ching or Rokudojikkyo, the Six Paramitastra). The second, a rendering of the Ramayana episode in which Dasharatha is cursed for accidentally killing a blind ascetic couple's son, is from a tenth-century collection of tales, the Sambo-ekotoba of MinamotonoTamenori, derived, no doubt, from the canonical version of the Sama Jataka. In addition to these Buddhist canonical sources, which inspired, it would seem, popular literary authors, Hara hypothesizes that the Rama story may have made its way into popular or courtly circulation directly from the oral versions narrated by Hindu savants, such as Bharadvaja Bodhisena, who were known to have visited Japan from the eighth century onwards (Hara 1983). In East Asia, as in the rest of the continent, the Ramayana story has been fully localized and naturalized and is rarely regarded as belonging to an exotic or alien culture.[122]

Hara provides a sincere interpretation of medieval Japanese literature in relation to the Ramayana's interpretations in the Far East. The first text she studies is the most prominent version of the Ramayana in Japan in the form of a collection of stories called the "Hobutsushu," which was written by TairanoYasoyori in the 12th Century. The second is an adaptation of a story from the Valmiki

Ramayana, in which king Dasharatha unwittingly commits the murder of a young ascetic, which foreshadows the tragic death of the king in his later days. Hara clarifies that the two works have come to Japan from India via China, in the shape of the Chinese Tripitaka. The story of the unnamed king in the Hobutsushu is as follows: There is a king of a peaceful and prosperous country referred to as "Tathagata Sakyamuni". This kingdom has a neighbor called "Kyushi," which is gripped with crippling famine and food shortage. Therefore, the people of Kyushi decide to declare war on Tathagata Sakyamuni to gain access to resources. The people of Tathagata Sakyamuni too begin to prepare for battle in defence of their homeland. However, the king of Tathagata Sakyamuni, as an avowed Buddhist cannot sanction such a war that would result in widespread loss of life. Therefore, he chooses to go into exile of his volition accompanied by his wife and begins life in the mountains. So, the episode of Lord Ram's exile in the Valmiki Ramayana is turned on its head, and there is no role of king Dasharatha and the battle for Ayodhya's throne between his wives and their aspirations for their sons.

One day however, the king and queen are visited by an ascetic who is impressed with the king's eschewal of worldly pleasures and professes his willingness to live with them. The royal couple agrees. But when the king went out to pick fruits, the ascetic abducts his wife and disappears. When the king returns, he discovers the ascetic's treachery and embarks on a journey to find his wife. On his journey, he finds a giant wounded bird. The bird informs the king of the ascetic's treachery and of its failed attempt to prevent the abduction. But the ascetic transforms into a "dragon-king" and injured the bird, breaking both of its wings. With these words, the bird breathed its last and was subsequently buried at the top of the mountain where the king lived. The episode involving the bird is similar to the Valmiki Ramayana but the nature of the ascetic's treachery is entirely modified, as there is no deception in the shape of a magical deer although Ravan or the "dragon-king" does shape-shift. As the king continues on his journey he encounters a large group of monkeys who have been left dispossessed of their homeland by a rival monkey clan. The king joins their war effort as an army general. This is a departure from the Buddhist ethics described earlier. The king is given a bow and arrows as weapons. His skills as an archer are unmatched and the enemy monkey clan is defeated. In return for his help, the monkeys agree to aid the king's efforts to find the dragon-king and rescue his wife.

In their journey, the king and his army of monkeys reach the southernmost tip of the kingdom. Their path is blocked by a large waterbody. Impressed with the king's adherence to Buddhist ethics, "Brahma Sakka" or god of the heavens in Buddhist cosmology (similar to Hindu god Indra), intercedes offering a way through. He tells the monkeys to "take a piece of timber and a handful of herbs, in order to make a bridge, and then to cross the bridge to the island, the mansion of the Dragon". The monkeys follow his advice and indeed begin such an undertaking, eventually crossing over to the dragon-king's realm. This episode of bridge-building too resonates with the Valmiki Ramayana, albeit the introduction of Brahma Sakka is unique to Buddhist interpretations and the means of building the bridge too are localised to Japan. The dragon-king is incensed by the arrival of the king and his monkey army to his realm. His attack paralyses the monkeys who grow intoxicated by the dew and frightened by the snow, eventually falling to the ground. One of the monkeys therefore makes a long journey to the tip of the Himalaya to gather "great herbs" to treat his brethren and revive them with powers greater than before. In the Japanese version, the monkeys collectively are injured by the dragon-king, and not Lakshmana at the hands of Ravan's son, as says the Valmiki Ramayana. And instead of Hanuman finding the Sanjivini Booti atop Mount Dronagiri, it is found by an ordinary monkey in the Himalayas. In the ensuing battle, the king's arrows are able to defeat the dragon-king and he rescues his wife from the latter's realm. At this time, the king of Kyushi has died, and the people of Tathagata Sakyamuni and Kyushi invite the king to rule over both kingdoms.

The second version of the Japanese Ramayana is referred to as the "Sambo-ekotoba," which is mainly an episodic account from the life of King Dasharatha. It was initially meant as an accompaniment to a series of paintings or "picture-scrolls". However, over time, the paintings were lost, but the written text endured. In certain versions of the Ramayana in India, this episode begins with a reference to King Dasharatha informing his wife "Kausalya" that his *"karma"* is responsible for his separation from his favoured son Lord Ram. King Dasharatha had accidentally struck a young ascetic with his arrow, only to be cursed by his blind parents of having to endure a similar fate of painful separation from his son in his old age. But the Japanese version in the Sambo-ekotoba has a twist towards the end. It is inspired by the Pali Jataka 540 or the Sama/Syamaka Jataka, which is part of the Buddhist text "Mahavastuavadana". In the Sambo-ekotoba, the young ascetic and his parents (who are described as rich merchants", hails from the city of "Kaira". They lose their eyesight because of their advanced age. They are therefore completely dependent on their son "Semu (also Zenshin)," who is a devout follower of the 10 Buddhist virtues and completely devoted to his duties of parental care. The rich merchants, acting in line with conventional Buddhist wisdom, proceed to donate all their material wealth to the poor and retire to the mountains. Semu builds for his parents a hermitage with a bed made of the "mugwort" plant. He would use the water from a nearby reservoir and pluck fruits and berries from the forest to sustain them. His sense of devotion to his parents was so extreme that the flora and fauna of the forest also developed an affection for his deeds.

One day however, he put on a cloak made of deer hide and proceeded to bring water for his parents. Incidentally, the reservoir where he was drawing water from was also being used by a herd of deer to drink water. At that moment, the king of Kaira was on a hunting expedition in the depths of a mountain (reference to King Dasharatha). He shot an arrow at the herd of deer, but inadvertently it struck Semu, who the king had mistaken for a deer. The king exclaimed: "Alas, I have committed a grievous sin, killing this noble son by mistake. I have incurred grave sin seeking a small pleasure. How could I ever cure your wound?" Even on his death bed, Semu consoled the king, blaming the karma from his previous life for his fate. In repentance, the king pledged to take care of Semu's parents in his stead. Upon hearing of their son's demise, the parents are un-consolable. They are brought to the spot at which Semu had died, and they appeal to the gods to revive their son as he had lived a life of "Buddha, Dharma, and Sangha". Sakka Brahma (god Indra) is moved by their appeal, and presents himself in human form to revive Semu by pouring "amrut" into his mouth. Sakka Brahma also cures his parents' blindness. This episodic reference to the Ramayana is used to impart Buddhist moral teachings. The king changes his ways and accepts a life of non-violence thereafter. He returns to his kingdom and proclaims: "those who take care of old blind parents as Semu does should be assisted by other people. On the contrary, those who injure devoted sons will incur heavy punishment". Thus, all over his kingdom people taught each other to act like Semu, keeping with the five commandments and practising the ten virtues (dharma); and after death they all were born in heaven, and nobody fell into hell".[123]

A modern Japanese perspective on the Ramayana is provided by Miki Sakae, a traveller who was inspired by his time in Thailand during the first half of the 20th Century. Upon his return to Japan, he published a book titled "Journey to the West [Ramakien] of Thailand" in 1961. He described the transmission of the Ramayana from India to other parts of Asia, including Thailand. Miki argued that the Ramayana had reached Khmer shores in Angkor—as was evident to him from archaeological relics—before the establishment of Sukhothai as an independent state. Miki claimed the Hindu epic had inspired the popular Japanese folktale "Momotaro," which is a "story of the son of a peach". It described as follows: Folk tales on the subject of "onitaiji" or exterminating demons have been told in Japan. Among them, most widely known is the story of Momotarō, who is said to have been born out of a peach, kills demons with the help of his loyal dog, pheasant, and monkey, who make up his entourage. This story contains motifs that partially overlap with Ramayana, and some believe that they are related. Certainly, it is possible to imagine some kind of influence in the story's motifs. Still, it cannot be considered that Ramayana itself as a long epic has taken root in Japan".

The National Museum of Ethnology in Japan also exhibits the Ramayana using performing arts (puppets and masks). Fukuoka Shota argues that "through the 20th century, the Japanese people's interest in Ramayana has increased". He believes that has coincided with an increased national appetite for Indian philosophy, which has been influenced by Japanese migration to other parts of South East Asia where the Ramayana was being performed in shadow puppet theatres and dances. Despite these progresses, the precise origins of the Ramayana in Japan are still unclear. Some scholars believe that the dances of toragaku depicted scenes from Ramayana and were popular between the 7th and 11th Century. Fukuoka adds that "there is also a theory that Ramayana was orally brought to Japan in the year 736 by the Buddhist monk Buttestu (Fozhe in Chinese) from Annam, who came to Japan accompanying Indian Monk Bodaisenna (Bodhisena). However, the tradition of toragaku was interrupted, and Ramayana was not transmitted to later generations". MinakataKumagusu wrote about references to the Ramayana in old Japanese books in 1914. After World War II, the circulation of the translated versions of the Ramayana from English in Japan increased significantly. Performances based on the Ramayana have also been popularised, as several Javanese artists, together with the Japanese, have begun to perform performing arts such as the wayangkulit.[124]

Chapter 10

Sri Lanka and Kumāradāsa's Janakiharana

The Ramayana is revered in Sri Lanka and holds a special place in the hearts of the Sinhalese population, who are predominantly Buddhists. Lord Ram is considered an exemplary figure, embodying virtues such as dharma (righteousness). His story is often used to illustrate moral and ethical lessons of Buddhism. The Ramayana is also an integral part of the cultural identity of Sri Lankan Tamils, who trace their origins to South India. The Hindu epic has played a crucial role in shaping Sri Lankan art, literature, and performing arts. Traditional dance and drama performances often feature episodes from the epic. The story has inspired a rich tradition of storytelling, with various adaptations and retellings in Sinhala literature. The epic has been a source of inspiration for poets, writers, and artists over centuries as Sri Lanka was believed to be the 'Lanka' mentioned in the Ramayana, where Sita was held captive by Ravan. This geographical identification seems to have been a late first-millennium South Indian innovation, later sustained by the kings of Jaffna.There is no evidence that the 'Lanka' of Valmiki's Ramayana was intended to correspond with the island of Sri Lanka. Yet, the site where Sita is said to have been held captive is identified as the Ashok Vatika in present-day Sri Lanka. Several places in Sri Lanka too are associated with events from the Ramayana, such as the Divurumpola, believed to be the location where Sita underwent the trial by fire (*Agni Pariksha*). The worship of Hindu deities, particularly Rama, Sita, and Hanuman, is prevalent in certain regions of Sri Lanka. Devotees visit temples dedicated to these figures, seeking blessings and guidance. The chanting of verses from the Ramayana, especially the "Sundara Kanda", is considered auspicious and is a common religious practice. While the Ramayana has deeply influenced Sri Lankan culture and society, it's important to note that interpretations and practices may vary across different communities and regions within the country. The epic continues to be a source of cultural and spiritual inspiration in Sri Lanka, contributing to the rich tapestry of the island country's heritage.

Whilst the Sanskrit versions of the Ramayana, and the Valmiki Ramayana are prominent in Sri Lanka, a poetic version of the text titled "Janakiharana" is a notable Sinhalese translation in the island country. The complete text of the Janakiharana consists of twenty cantos, containing a total number of 1,452 stanzas together with 509 stanzas which are considered to be interpolations. It was authored by the Sinhalese poet Kumāradāsa, and is an episodic reference to Sita's abduction by Ravan. As per popular folklore, Sri Lankans believe Kumāradāsa is King Kumāradhātusena (513–522 A.D.) of Sri Lanka. As C.E. Godakumbura tell us, "in 1852, James D'Alwis, in his introduction to the "Sidath Sangarawa," ascribed the authorship of the Janakiharana to King Kumāradāsa of Ceylon, basing his evidence on the stanza of the "Pärākum – bāsirita", and related here the story of the tragic end of the king and his friend, the poet Kālidāsa. D'Alwis has also added the Sinhalese lines popularly connected with the event, with an English translation of the same".[125] Indeed, the influence of the Indian poet Kalidasa is quite evident in the Janakiharana. As Chittenjoor Kunhan Raja has argued, "in language, in the metres that he adopts, in the descriptions, in the entire technique of the epic, the influence which Kālidāsa must have exerted on the poet is quite plain...he is quite original in his presentation of the theme...He must have been a great scholar and grammarian.... he is never pedantic in his use of the language. He ranks as among the best poets, and in tradition, he is brought into an equal position with Kālidāsa and Raghuvaṃśa".[126] Theodor Aufrecht, first brought the text of the Janakiharan to the attention of scholars in 1859, as part of an edited volume titled the "Ujjvalàdatta's commentary on the Uṇādis".[127] In addition, "Aufrecht in an article on the "*Śarngadharapaddhati*" which he contributed to the ZDMG, XVII, traced two stanzas from Kumāradāsa which were later traced to the Janakiharana".[128]

Susantha Goonatilake conjectures that the transmission of the Ramayana to Sri Lanka occurred quite late despite the proximity of Sri Lanka to India: "Hindu gods feature first occurs during the Cola invasion in Polona two Śiva devales, but there are no depictions of the Ramayana".the Ramayana comes much later to Sri Lanka when Hindu influences occurred, especially during the Gampola–Kotte period Buddhist literature (15th Century)".[129] There is surprisingly no Sinhalese or Tamil vernacular version of the Ramayana in Sri Lanka. Even the Pali Chronicles (Dipavamsa and

Mahavamsa) do not make mention of the Hindu epic, which is unlike the spread of the Ramayana via Buddhist intermediaries in other parts of Asia. Heinz Bechert has argued that this was because "the Mahavihara writers of early Pali chronicles consciously excluded any narrative from the Ramayana in order to preserve the primacy of Sinhala Buddhist political and religious life on the island".[130] Richard Gombrich on the other hand, speculates that "the absence of the Ramayana in Pali historiography reflects Theravada Buddhist hostility towards its Brahmanical Hindu values".[131] Steven Collins has suggested that "the Pali Vessantara Jataka was able to serve as a substitute for the Ramayana in Sri Lanka because it is made up of the same basic story matrix".[132] The battle between Lord Ram and Ravan has also been one that political opportunists have historically defined as a contest between Aryan North India and the Dravidian South. This affected the Ramayana's reception in parts of South India, and beyond, where Dravidian culture and identity permeated: "the Dravidian movement of the early twentieth century, for instance, rejected the Ramayana altogether, while others attempted to elevate Ravan to the status of a great historical figure—virtuous ruler and ardent devotee of Siva".

However, Justin W. Henry and Sree Padma, have argued that such scholars have "overlooked…the routine presence of Ramayana characters, imagery and narrative motifs in Sinhala Buddhist poetry and historical works, in the architecture and ritual life of Buddhist viharas (temples), as well as in the myths associated with the founding of some of Sri Lanka's most significant Hindu temples". They particularly emphasise the influence of Kumāradāsa's

Janakiharana after the 5th Century as evidence of the Ramayana's imprint on Sinhalese literature.[133] There is also a rejection of the Ramayana's importance by the 5th Century "Sri Lankan commentator Buddhaghosa," who twice refersto Sita's abduction as a 'pointless story'. The geographical identification of Sri Lanka as Ravan's Lanka takes place around the 8th Century in Southern India, and is "contained in the Kasakudi plates of Nandivarman". It boasts of king Narasimhavarman I having surpassed Lord Ram due to his capture of Lanka. This political and cultural significance was also mobilised during the Chola Empire, as they began making military headway on the island in the early 10th century. Similar self-congratulatory references are available at the Citamparam Siva temple complex and the Udayendram plates of Prthvipati II (c. 919 CE). The Tiruvalangadu plates of Rajendra (c. 1017 CE) capture the utility of Lanka's symbolism in demonising the enemies of the Chola Empire:

> Constructing a bridge across the water of the ocean with the assistance of able monkeys, the Lord of the Raghavas (i.e. Rama) killed with great difficulty the king of Lanka (i.e. Ravana) with sharp-edged arrows—[but] this terrible general of his (the general of King Rajaraja, Rajendra's father) crossed the ocean with ships and burnt the Lord of Lanka. Hence Rama is surpassed by him (i.e. by Rajendra).[134]

Despite these inroads, it is clear that the influence of the Ramayana achieved a sizeable proportion in the island country only in the 14th Century, with the increased dominance of Southern Indian kingdoms on Sinhala Buddhist folklore, literature and temple life in particular.

Henry and Padma attribute this phenomenon to: "(1) the emerging independent Tamil kingdom of Jaffna; (2) a change in composition among the ruling elites of the island's southwest (with two prominent royal families of this era being of Malayali extraction); and (3) at the level of the overall demographics of the island, with Sri Lanka's south and southwest absorbing a sizeable influx of immigrants from the southern subcontinent from the fourteenth century onwards".Later, there were texts such as the "VaiyaPadal", a 16thCentury chronicle of the kingdom of Jaffna, as well as the YalppanaVaipava Malai from the 18th Century, that begin their narration of the island's history with Lord Rammaking Vibhishana the king of Lanka. Eventually, the Ramayana was able to cater to the political and cultural needs of Sri Lanka's Tamil Saiva and Sinhala Buddhist population across centuries.[135]

The favourable view of Ravan in thc Sri Lankan Tamil tradition is notable. There is a story known as the "Ravana anugraha murti" in the Sanskrit Puranas and Agamas, which reads as follows:

> Ravan was flying through the air on his chariot when his route was blocked by Mount Kailasa. Arrogantly, he uprooted the mountain and began to toss it aside. Siva intervened, pinning Ravan beneath the mountain. After a thousand years of being trapped thus, which he spent singing hymns of Siva's majesty in apology, Ravan was released by Siva, who blessed him with a boon (in some versions consisting of long life, in others an invincible sword, in others a lingam to worship).

However, Sri Lankan Tamils have portrayed Ravan sympathetically as an ardent devotee of god Shiva. Hence, "in the temple literature of Koneswaram, the sentiment of Ravana anugraha murti is inverted, making Ravan's feat of lifting Mount Kailasa an act of extreme heroism and piety (rather than an act of arrogance)". The yaksa king (unlike *'raksasa'* which meant demon, *yaksas* are identified in Buddhist cosmology as the guardians of shrines) Ravan is seen as the originator of the Sinhala nation in some sense, even prior to Prince Vijaya (the first king of the island and progenitor of the Sinhala Buddhist people, according to the Mahavamsa). In fact, "The Maddakkalappu Purva Carittiram", which is a Tamil history of Batticaloa from the 18th Century, explicitly traces Lankan monarchy from Ravan's reign to the arrival of Prince Vijaya, claiming that Lord Ram had remained to rule Lanka instead of returning to Ayodhya after the battle. Sri Lankan Tamils embraced the reference of Sri Lanka as the 'Lanka' from the Valmiki Ramayana, but they subverted the pejorative logic of Southern Indian kingdoms and their Chola predecessors. Instead, they "remembered [Ravan] for his piety and foundational role at places of Saiva worship across the island". This adulation of Ravan was exemplified by the 17th CenturySetupati rulers of Ramnad and Sivaganga. Notably, in Kandyan-period poetry, the Sinhalese make mention of era of the demon-king's reign as the 'Ravan yuga'.[136] There is also a fabled a 17th or 18th Century poem, the Ravana Kathava, which speaks of the Ramayana from Ravan's perspective:

> Ravan's relationship with his brothers is the subject of considerable dialogue, the conflagration of Lanka is described in extended detail, and the agony of Ravan upon seeing his kingdom ruined casts the demon-king as an almost tragic victim. Ravan is described as 'one

possessing great merit' and in an impassioned plea from his brother Kumbhakarna imploring him not to go to war with Rama, the virtuous deeds of his life are recounted.

Henry argues that there are also other medieval Sinhalese poems that highlight Ravan's fairness, and instead present Lord Ram as the aggressor: "it is explained that Ravan abducted Sita purely in retaliation for Lord Ram and Lakshmana's violence against his sister Surpanakha, not out of lust or intemperance". Not only was this in light of Ravan's provenance being linked to 'Lanka,' but it was also a conscious effort from Buddhist scholars to downplay the divinity of Hindu gods, such as Vishnu. Hindu gods were important in the island country's folklore but had to assume a stature subordinate to Lord Buddha to retain Buddhism's prominence.

The other important character of special relevance to Sri Lanka from the Ramayana is Vibhishana. His reference is first found inthe 14th Century Gampola, which has intended to represent the symbolic subjugation of southwestern Lankan regents to the Vijayanagar Empire.[137] Sree Padma has carried out a detailed study of the history and significance of Vibhishana in the island country. She begins her examination at the famous Vibhishana cult shrine in Sri Lanka at a temple in Kelaniya. Here, "Vibhishana stands next to Saman, another of the satara varan devi (four warrant or guardian deities of the island), in the company of a host of other *devas* and *dikpalas* (rulers of various divisions of the world). These colourful paintings adorn the walls, with Vibhishana depicted as a yaksa/raksasa (giant/demon) with red eyes and protruding teeth gazing at the reclining Buddha". The depiction demonstrates the variegated associations of Vibhishana to the Hindu epic, the island, and Lord Buddha (yatikas all depict Vibhishana as a bodhisattva or future Buddha).Vibhishana achieves exalted status in medieval Sri Lanka and true assimilation into Buddhism when he is first mentioned as "one of the four 'god kings' (devirajjuruvan) of the island, alongside Saman (Sumana), Ganesha (Ganapati) and Skanda, in a 1344 inscription at the Lankatilaka Vihara at Gampola". The inscription is in Sinhalese as well as Tamil. One of the local adaptations of the Ramayana claims that his promotion to the pantheon of gods occurs due to Vibhishana'sgovernance being aligned with the"Dasaraja Dharma"as he made Kelaniya his capital city. His legacy becomes ossified as the guardian deity and overlord of Sri Lanka and Sinhalese Buddhist rulers. As per the folklore of Kelaniya temple, Vibhishana became ruler of a region called "Maya Rata" in his lifetime, which had sunk due to Ravan's unethical behaviour. In some versions of Sinhalese Buddhist literature, Vibhishana is considered diminished in valour in comparison to Ravan, but he is credited with (albeit controversial) Ravan's downfall and death for his evil deeds (not Lord Ram), and is perceived as saving Lanka from chaos afterwards.[138]

Chapter 11

Nepal and the Bhanubhakta Ramayana

> The Ramayana, Mahabharata and religious epics do not only contribute to the enhancement of language, literature and culture but also help people's sense of religion, spiritualism, socialization, morality and the notion of simple living high thinking.
>
> —Nepali Vice President Ram Sahay Prasad Yadav[139]

As a predominantly Hindu country, the Ramayana is considered a sacred scripture in Nepal. The values and principles depicted in the Hindu epic are deeply ingrained in the religious consciousness of the Nepalese people. The Ramayana is central to many Hindu festivals celebrated in Nepal. Dashain, one of the major festivals in the country, involves the recitation of the Ramayana and the enactment of scenes from the Hindu epic. During Tihar (the festival of lights), people worship animals, including crows, dogs, and cows, inspired by the characters in the Ramayana. The Ramayana has also provoked various forms of traditional Nepalese art, including paintings, sculptures, and dance forms. Many temples and palaces in Nepal feature carvings depicting scenes from the Ramayana. It has also been a source of inspiration for Nepalese literature, with poets and writers drawing upon its themes and narratives in their works. Several places in Nepal are believed to be associated with events from the Ramayana. Janakpur, for example, is believed to be the birthplace of Sita and is an important pilgrimage site for Hindus, and the key site of Lord Ram's worship in modern Nepal. Pilgrims often follow routes that are associated with the journey of Lord Ram, such as the Muktinath Temple in Mustang. In fact, Nepali Prime Minister Khadga Prasad Sharma Oli had claimed in 2020 that an obscure Nepali village called Thori, west of Birgunj, and not Ayodhya, was the birthplace of Lord Ram.[140] Then he ordered archaeologists to start excavations near Thori looking for signs of Lord Ram, while local officials were instructed to erect 'massive' statues of Lord Ram, Sita and Lakshman for Ram Nawami celebrations.[141]

A version of the Ramayana titled the "Nepal Bhasa Ramayana," is a Nepalese retelling of the ancient Hindu epic in the Nepali language written by Siddhidas Mahaju, and it reflects the cultural and regional variations of Nepal. While the core narrative follows the story of Lord Rama, Sita, and Hanuman, the Nepali version does incorporate local traditions, beliefs, and customs. One notable aspect of the Nepali Ramayana is the influence of the Newar community, an indigenous ethnic group in the Kathmandu Valley of Nepal. The Newar people have their own cultural traditions and language (Nepal Bhasa or Newari), and their version of the Ramayana includes unique elements and interpretations. The Nepali Ramayana has been transmitted through oral traditions, storytelling, and various literary works in

Nepal Bhasa. It plays a significant role in the cultural and religious life of the people in Nepal, contributing to the rich tapestry of the country's folklore and religious narratives. The storytelling of the Ramayana is often accompanied by traditional music, dance, and drama, further enriching its cultural expression in Nepal. The Ramayana traditions of Nepal visible during the celebration of the Vivaha Panchami and the Ram Nawami festivals, and also during the Gai Jatra festival, "a day when the dead are remembered, and children from families with recently deceased members dress up as various mythological figures, including the quartet of Ram, Sita, Lakshman and Hanuman".[142]

The other prominent Nepali version of the Ramayana was authored by Bhanubhakta Acharya (1814–1868), who was a revered poet and writer from the Central hills of Nepal in the village of Ramgha in Tanhun, and is best known for translating the Ramayana into the Nepali language. His version is commonly known as the "Bhanubhakta Ramayana" and is written in a lucid manner and easy-flowing verses, with a free rendering of the slokas (metrical stanzaic forms) into arrestingly rhythmic *bhasa* (Nepali)[143]. Bhanubhakta Acharya is referred to as *"aadikavi"*, meaning the "first poet", in Nepali literature. Bhanubhakta Acharya's translation of the Ramayana, also referred to as "aadi kavya," is considered a seminal work in Nepali literature as it made the Hindu epic more accessible to Nepali people. Although a translation, the Nepali people consider it be an original composition in many respects. The main motifs remain the same as the Valmiki Ramayana, but the episodes are condensed. At various junctures, he has also introduced local elements to suit the

Nepali readership. Lord Ram is portrayed as a more human character rather than having god-like abilities. Sita is also shown as a more prominent and courageous character, who strongly rebuffs Ravan's advances and enticements whilst in captivity. The character of Bharat, Lord Ram's brother, is shown in a noble light, even to an extend of redeeming the ill acts of his mother Kaikeyi. Ravan is shown in a somewhat favourable light, and is praised for his restraint in dealing with Sita in captivity.

Bhanubhakta Acharya's contribution to Nepali literature is commemorated annually on his birthday, known as Bhanu Jayanti. During this day, events and programs are organized to celebrate his life and works, and excerpts from the Bhanubhakta Ramayana may be recited. The Bhanubhakta Ramayana is an adaptation of the "Sanskrit Adhvatma Ramayana," which is a dialogue between *"Bhaktivada"* and *"Atmavada"*. Bhanubhakta Acharya was evidently more influenced by the Bhakti tradition of the Ramayana, whilst also being a devotee of Atmavada interpretations. Due to his translation of the Ramayana, he achieved an almost god-like stature in Nepali society. Pratyoush Onta explicates the relevance of Acharya Bhanubhakta for Nepali nationalism:

> As Nepali nationalists love to point out, Bhanubhakta is said to have effected the emotional unification of all Nepalis, that is, those brought together inside territorial Nepal by King Prithvinarayan Shah, through his rendering of Ramayana into colloquial Nepali. Literary history pivoting around Bhanubhakta, and celebrations (in various modes) of Bhanubhakta as the second 'unifier' of Nepal via the medium of the Nepali language are two important aspects of the dominant national culture.[144]

Amish Raj Mulmi argues that this claim is mistaken as "it was in British India's Benares and Darjeeling that Nepali language activists first co-opted Bhanubhakta as a Nepali icon". But this has not stifled the rise of Bhanubhakta's legend in Nepali folklore. Mulmi traces the worship of Lord Ram in Nepal as far back as 608 CE to a "Licchavi inscription in Hadigaon, one of Kathmandu Valley's oldest settlements". Thereafter, more and more evidence came up: "an 11th Century manuscript in a Nepalbhasa script, written for an official named Anandadeva by a Tirhuti Kayastha, is considered to be one of the oldest versions of the epic. The image of Hanuman, Ram's most famous devotee, at the Hanuman Dhoka was erected in 1672 CE by Pratap Malla, and several friezes in the 17th-century Krishna Temple in Patan show scenes from the Ramayana. Another manuscript in a Nepalbhasa script from the 17th-century, like the older one, is part of the critical edition of Valmiki's Ramayana. Themes from Ram's life were also featured in a 15th-century manuscript cover.[145]

Mulmi's examination into the origins of the Ramayana in Nepal shows that it is the worship of god Vishnu that gained currency in the country, rather than that of Lord Ram. He argues that the Vaishnavite Malla kings, who were the ruling dynasty of the Kathmandu Valley in Nepal from 1201 to 1779, leaned towards the worship of Lord Krishna, and even his Narasimha form, instead of Lord Ram. Later, The Shah kings, also known as the Shahs of Gorkha or the Royal House of Gorkha, and were the ruling Chaubise Thakuri dynasty and the founders of the Gorkha Kingdom from 1559 onwards, "too, with their martial backgrounds, did not seem to valorise the story of Lord Ram, even as they incorporated the epic in their architectures, such as in the Nautale Durbar in Kathmandu, built under Prithvi Narayan Shah himself, albeit following the prevailing Malla pagoda style". Mulmi argues that none of the popular Indian variants of the Ramayana, including Tulsi Das' fabled Ramcharitmanas, were prevalent in Nepal until the 19th Century. This view is corroborated by N R Banerjee: "even the cult image of Rama as an avatara of Vishnu is not much to be met with in the early, or medieval, art of Nepal, on the basis of the evidence that is presently available, despite the fact of the capital of Rajarshi Janaka Siradhvaja, father of Sita, being located at Janakpur".[146]

Another interesting facet in the story of the Ramayana in Nepal is the emergence of Janakpur as the mythical Mithila's capital from the Hindu epic, which also took place as late as the 18th Century. It is explained in the anthropologist Richard Burghart's 1978 essay "The disappearance and reappearance of Janakpur"[147]:

> During the sixteenth and seventeenth centuries of the present age, as the worship of Ram and the discipline of devotion spread throughout the Ganges basin, Hindu ascetics of the Ramanandi sect began to search for the places which during the Treta Yuga had been purified by the lotus feet of their Lord and Saviour, Ram Candra [sic]... Until the end of the seventeenth century, however, the site of Janakpur had not been discovered. For the Vaisnavite devotees Janakpur existed in their minds as an object of devotion and meditation, but janakpurdham, or the "site of Janakpur", remained unknown.

The mythical Janakpur, Mithila's capital, is said to have disappeared during the Kurukshetra war, and the Vaidehi dynasty went extinct. Burghart records oral traditions

> where Hindu ascetics Caturbhuj Giri of the Dasnami sect and Sur Kisor of the Ramanandi sect dreamt of Ram and Sita respectively, telling them where the modern site of Janakpur was. To Sur Kisor is attributed the verse that 'discovered' Shiva's bow in Dhanusa – "[t]welve miles north of Janakpur, where lies a forest". Subsequently, other Ramanandi ascetics built upon these lores, and 'discovered' Sitamarhi, the birthplace of Sita, and other modern-day shrines associated with the epic.
>
> Rather than actually discovering the site of ancient Janakpur, Caturbhuj Giri and Sur Kisor might have only confirmed a local tradition associating the site with Janakpur and then spread the renown of this sacred place to other pilgrimage centres in the Ganges basin.

Despite its proximity and shared religious foundations of Hinduism, Nepal has repelled the wholesale import of Sanskritised versions of the Ramayana to resist India's hegemonic cultural influence, which was possibly seen as threatening, or at the very least challenging, the exceptionality of Nepali cultural identity and the legitimacy of its political rulers across time. It is truly remarkable that the transmission and local adaptation of the Ramayana was easier in geographies where Indian rulers could not reach. It is unsurprising therefore that Darjeeling-based Nepali language activists in the 1920s rediscovered Bhanubhakta as a potent icon for their national project and "as an essential element of a unifying historical narrative for their own self-identity as a community". For instance, Poet Dharanidhar Koirala, a brahman from Dumjha in the eastern hilly district of Sindhuli of Nepal, published Bhanubhakta's name in the pages of the Candrika magazine in 1918. In 1920, he published a collection of poems called "Naivedhya" in which

Bhanubhakta's poems were also reprinted.Bhanubhakta, who had translated the Ramayana into Nepali language, was painted as a national hero for eschewing Sanskrit writing, which was in vogue at the time. Another member of Nepali literary circles in Benares, was Suryabikram Gyawali. Gyawali wrote:

> Like Bhanubhakta, let us disperse knowledge amongst our population through our mother-language. Knowledge is power and energy and light that destroys darkness... If we cannot see and understand the greatness [of Bhanubhakta] the fault lies with us...Just because our confused and educationless statusdoes not give us a good clear view [of our past] we cannot say Bhanubhakta was not good, not important. Bhanubhakta was good, he was big, he was majestic and since we lack those qualities we have not been able to appreciate his greatness. But time will give us eyes [to see those qualities], power to evaluate [them] and minds to understand Bhanubhakta. After that we will honour Bhanubhakta [properly] and understand his importance.

Bhanubhakta's status as a nationalist figure in Nepal suggests that the introduction of the Ramayana in Nepal, somewhat akin to Sri Lanka, has been complicated by the political and cultural expediencies of the Himalayan country and Nepalese society.The first public celebration of Bhanubhakta's birth took place in Darjeeling in 1945. Since then, the Nepali Sahitya Sammelan has held an annual event in Bhanubhakta's memory. As Pratyoush Onta has argued, "Bhanubhakta was a "birpurus" for having brought about the cultural unification of the Nepali [nation] through his Nepali language Ramayana"[148] For Nepali nationalists, it is in his adaption and localisation of an Indian-Hindu epic that Bhanubhakta becomes a figure of resistance against that very Indian-Hindu civilisation and the fulcrum of a modern Nepali national identity. In another article, Onta has conclusively shown that "Bhanubhakta's central location in Nepali national culture according to dominant national history—Bhanubhakta as the Nepali ādikavi and Bhanubhakta as the second unifier of all Nepalis".[149] He calls this process the hyper-nationalisation of Bhanubhakta in Nepal. The Bhanubhakta Ramayana, in the shape of its author, has become a national symbol and culture that, in its distinctiveness, animatesthe Nepali national identity.

Chapter 12

Ramlila in the Diaspora:

Reflections on Southall, North Carolina, and Trinidad and Tobago

> One of the first big public things I was taken to was the Ramlila, the pageant-play based on the Ramayana, the epic about the banishment and later triumph of Rama, the Hindu hero-divinity… Everything in that Ramlila has been transported from India in the memories of people. And although as theatre it was crude, and there was much that I would have missed in the story, I believe I understood more and felt more than I had done during The Prince and the Pauper... at the local cinema…the Ramayana was the essential Hindu story.
>
> —V. S. Naipaul[150]

> … It was as if, on the edge of the Central plain, there was another plateau, a raft on which the Ramayana would be poorly performed in this ocean of cane, but that was my writer's view of things, and it was wrong. I was seeing the Ramleela at Felicity as theatre when it was faith… They were not amateurs but believers… They believed in what they were playing, in the sacredness of the text.
>
> —Nobel Prize acceptance speech of Derek Walcott[151]

The Ramayana has also permeated the lives of India's Hindu diaspora, providing a narrative thread that connects individuals to their heritage and facilitates the preservation of cultural values. One of the primary ways in which the Ramayana has influenced the Indian diaspora is by serving as a repository of cultural continuity. Through the retelling of the epic, whether in the form of religious ceremonies, theatrical performances, or literary works, diasporic communities maintain a connection with their roots. The Ramayana, with its universal themes of righteousness, duty, and devotion, resonates across generations and geographical boundaries, offering a shared cultural heritage that binds the diaspora together. The Ramayana, is not merely an epic, but also a sacred scripture for millions of Hindus. As the Indian diaspora has settled in various parts of the world, the Ramayana has served as a spiritual anchor, providing a moral and ethical framework for individuals navigating the complexities of life in a foreign land. Temples and community gatherings often incorporate recitations and discussions of the Ramayana, fostering a sense of spiritual community and grounding diasporic populations in their religious traditions.

The Ramayana's influence extends beyond religious and cultural practices into the realms of literature, art, and popular culture. Many members of the Indian diaspora have sought to express their cultural identity through creative endeavours that draw inspiration from the epic. Whether through novels, poems, paintings, or films, the Ramayana serves as a wellspring of inspiration, allowing individuals to explore and reinterpret their cultural heritage in diverse and dynamic ways. In addition to providing a cultural and spiritual foundation, the Ramayana contributes to social cohesion within the Indian diaspora. Shared knowledge of the Hindu epic creates a sense of commonality and belonging, fostering community bonds that transcend regional, linguistic, and generational differences. The retelling of the Ramayana becomes a communal activity, reinforcing a collective identity that helps diasporic individuals navigate the challenges of assimilation while preserving their cultural distinctiveness. In this chapter, I briefly explore the celebration of the Ramayana, via its most popular dramatic folk re-enactment, i.e. the Ramlila in India's Hindu diaspora.

As Paula Richman's pioneering work shows us, one of the cities in which the performance of the Ramlila is popular is Southall, Greater London. Richman reminds us that the women of South Asian and African Caribbean descent—comprising of teenage school girls to young postgraduates and working women famously referred to as the Southall Black Sisters (SBS)—performed the Ramlila in in response to the incidents of 23 April 1979, to fund the legal costs for members of the community arrested in the demonstrations against the Neo-Nazi National Front. Their rendition of the Ramlila specifically adopted by the Southall Black Sisters used the figure of Lord Ram to fight their social ills. As Richman explains:

> ...[they] framed and periodically interrupted their rendition of the Ramlila with humorous commentary that gave a topical slant to the story's events, relating them to racism, socio-economic conditions in their area, local and national politics, and sexism. The character playing Ravan, king of the demons, wore a huge mask on which each of his ten heads had been drawn to represent an aspect of the racism that Black groups in Britain encountered in addition to heads bearing pictures of conservative politicians and neo-Nazi leaders, additional heads bore the insignia of the riot police and an image standing

> for immigration restrictions. The Ramlila performance culminated with the burning of the ten-headed effigy while audience members cheered.

One of the reasons behind the choice of the Ramayana as the choice of text for the performance was its galvanizing symbolic effect on the local Hindu community. It allowed the women of the Southall Black Sisters to show their solidarity with Hindu traditions whilst simultaneously using the tropes of virtuous and moral conduct as well as the need to mobilise and fight against social ills, including those plaguing xenophobic electoral politics in the U.K. as well as demands for social reforms within the local community against sexism. Therefore, "members of SBS chose, therefore, to stage a unique Ramlila, one that would combine cultural appreciation with cultural critique". For instance, unlike many of the performances of the Ramlila in India, all the characters of the epic were played by women. Additionally, there was guided narration to shed light on issues facing the women in the community. Richman explains further how the Ramayana was performed as a call for reform:

> The narrator tells us that when, after many childless years, Dasharatha performed a special religious sacrifice, his three wives became pregnant and gave birth to male children. What a great celebration the king sponsored! Here the first jester interrupted: "Yes it was like that when my brother was born-a great celebration and my family passed out laddhus. But when I was born, they didn't celebrate. My mother said "Hi Veh Raba, sootamundiyandhathaba". ...Now [members of the community] understood, thanks to the Panjabi comment of the first jester, that the dialogue called attention to the greater value placed on male babies than females, a fact of

life with which they were all too familiar.

In another scene where Lord Ram informs Sita that she need not accompany him during exile as it would cast an unfair burden on her, she:

> ...hits him in the shoulder with a thump and [asks], "I'm good enough to wear myself out doing all the house-work in our home, but not good enough to go to the forest with you?"

This response was one again followed by the intervention of a jester who questioned the heavy responsibilities of women having to work at the local T'walls Factory whilst also being held unfairly responsible for the performance of all domestic chores. The male characters in the performance were also made to appear short, weak, and occasionally coward-like. Ravan's death is seen as signifying the triumph of good over racism and other social ills of British society afflicting migrants from the Global South.[152] Another Ramlila performance that has received scholarly attention is that of The Hindu Society of North Carolina. Afroz Taj and John Caldwell have stated that the "Ramlila has been performed for the past ten years, on the occasion of Dussehra in the suburban town of Morrisville, North Carolina (population approximately 25,000)". They highlight however that "as community cultural activities and less as extended acts of worship". They too describe their version of the Ramlila as evolving to actively use the force of tradition to attend to gender disparities:

> It brings beloved characters to life and lets them speak for themselves, albeit through dubbing. The characters' motivations are explored in relatively long monologues, and there are gestures toward some of the moral

> complexities of the story. Most of the female characters are portrayed as thinking subjects with a large degree of agency. Sita, in particular, is presented as a strong, complex character whose emotions run the gamut from despair to anger. The Ramlila's three-section structure provides something for everyone: dance-drama, formal drama, and spectacular fireworks. Through it, the organizers seek to further the dual religious and cultural objectives of the Hindu community while simultaneously promoting Indian and Hindu culture to a broader audience.[153]

One of the lesser known countries in which the Ramlila is exceedingly popular amongst the Hindu community is Trinidad and Tobago. Kumar Mahabir and Susan Chand explain the historical roots of the large Hindu community in Trinidad: "between 1838 and 1917, more than half a million Indians were transported to the Caribbean as indentured labourers after the abolition of formal slavery in 1834 by the British Empire. India was a suitable source of cheap labour for the colonial planters because of the large population with the majority of its inhabitants accustomed to agricultural labour and similar climatic conditions as those of the Caribbean. Moreover, negotiations for immigration to the Caribbean were easy as these were facilitated by the British who were in control of both colonies". About 85% of these indentured labourers and migrants in Trinidad were Hindus, as they were recruited primarily from north Indian states such as "Bihar (14 per cent), Oudh (part of present-day Uttar Pradesh and Uttarakhand, 24-8 per cent) and North-west Provinces (currently part of Uttar Pradesh, 48-52 per cent)". In the difficult tenor of their life as labourers, cultural traditions and community activities offered a much-needed respite. Consequently, the Ramayana and its theatrical folk performance in the shape of the Ramlila assumed great social significance, especially during the celebration of the Hindu festival of Diwali. Since there were no temples as such in Trinidad during the early phase of indentured migration, the Ramlila became the closest approximation of a pilgrimage for the labourers.

Mahabir and Chand arguc that it was Tulsidas' Ramcharitmanas from the Bhakti tradition that was most popular in rural areas in the Caribbean, having been bought in textual form or as an oral tradition. Amazingly, "the earliest documented record of Ramlila in Trinidad can be traced back to 1880 in Dow Village, California, in Central Trinidad. 'Dow Village Ramlila' has an unbroken history of over 135 years of performance". Its first performance was rendered in the Bhojpuri language. This particular Ramlila takes place in an open area in the village recreational park. There is also another famous Ramlila festival in the country, which is the second oldest Ramlila celebration known as the 'Chaguanas Ramlila.' It later came to be known as the 'First Felicity Ramlila'. There are also other famous Ramlila celebrations such as the 'Maha Sabha Ramlila' of Felicity and the 'Pierre Road Ramlila' in Charlieville (located north-east of the First Felicity Ramlila). Notably, the Ramlila tradition is unique to Trinidad and Tobago, despite the population of Hindus being higher in neighbouring Guyana. This may be due to the coincidentally stronger nature of transmission of the Ramayana in Trinidad. Usually, labourers did not carry significant belongings with them, including religious texts. But in Trinidad, "when they came to the Caribbean, they brought not only the memory of the Ramayana but the continuity of language, music, rhythms, religion, and a strong oral tradition". The Ramlila performance in Trinidad takes place in the "Lokadharma" dramatic style, wherein performers mime the dialogues. As per Mahabir and Chand, currently "Ramlila performances are held in over 35 venues across Trinidad" by respective local committees and the festivities typically run for 10–11 days and culminate with the burning of Ravan's effigy, occasionally accompanied by his brother Kumbhakaran, and his son Meghnath.[154]

In Trinidad and Tobago, Hindus who performed as part of the Ramlila did so for personality development and to be educated about their religious roots. Its prominence is only further evidenced by the fact that politicians in Trinidad use the Ramlila as an opportunity to curry favourable electoral support from the Hindu communities. A local community worker called Ravindra Nath Maharaj describes the significance of the Ramayana for the Indo-Trinidadians at length:

> In moving, Ram claimed and was claimed by the land itself, not only Ayodhya but the forest in which he lived out his exile and Ravan's kingdom of Lanka where, by proxy, he established the first Ramraj through the rule of Bibheeshan. In Trinidad, instead of returning to India, we made a new vernacular Ayodhya, signified by the term "Ramdilla". In that context Ramdilla allowed for almost all the traditions to be practiced together: the singing tradition, the kathaa tradition [telling the story], the paath tradition [ritual recitation], the art of interpreting in several languages at the same time. Faced with having to claim space, speaking to the issues which our people faced under colonialism, and making an independent Trinidad and Tobago, we found our own David and Goliath in Ram and Ravan, in the people and the colonial power. The continual offering of citizenship in our own

> Ayodhya is the way we express our kind of patriotism, our love for our Nation, which we can only do in this way. The process of our being citizens here, as Ramayana people, had to come from the Manas. It reconciled being there, maintaining ties to India, and being here simultaneously. The Tulsidas Manas—itself written in the vernacular—already provided the model. Sublimating the pain, aware of our isolation, the cosmic journey also became our local story. This is the political dimension for us of the Ramayana.

The Ramayana ends with Lord Ram and Sita returning to Ayodhya. But as Milla Riggio argues, "it would seem that here the parallel with the Trinidad story ends, for the Indo-Trinidadians who remained, without returning. In a deeper sense, this is why the persona of Lord Ram is a revelation to the Indo-Trinidadians as his "humble acceptance of exile finally leads him home"—something of great significance for the Indo-Trinidadians, especially in the earlier phases of indenture. The Ramayana and the Ramlila therefore are a part of the self-discovery of the Indo-Trinidadian identity and provided a socio-cultural anchor to satisfy the tensions created by their "state of in-betweenity" as a diasporic community.[155]Relatedly, Sherry Ann Singh has argued that the Ramayana tradition in Trinidad "by constantly informing and reflecting the Trinidad Hindu experience, can be deemed both mirror and metaphor of history and society, and thus, Hindu socio-religious transformation". For instance, the physical depiction of Ravan during the Ramlila has transitioned based on the physical description of evil at the time, whether it was "white colonial oppressors, the Africans, the negative impact of Western elements, or any other more palpable threatening agents such as drugs, violence or criminal activity". At times, the character of Ravan has also been shown with a darker complexion to indicate the dissatisfaction of the Hindu community with the Afro–Trinidadian political elite.[156]

Overall, the performance of the Ramlila in various diasporic communities shows the continuing influence and relevance of the Ramayana in India's diaspora, and is a testament to the enduring power of cultural narratives to shape and sustain identity. As members of the Hindu diaspora traverse the globe, the Ramayana continues to serve as a bridge between the past and the present, offering a timeless and universal message that resonates across borders. Through religious practices, literary expressions, and artistic endeavours, the Ramayana remains a vibrant and integral part of the lives of the Hindu diaspora, reinforcing a shared sense of heritage and cultural pride. In this way, the Hindu epic continues to enrich the lives of individuals and communities, ensuring that the spirit of the Ramayana endures across generations and geographical distances.

Conclusion

Return of Lord Ram to Ayodhya

Across the twelve chapters in this book I have explored how the story of the Ramayana, the fabled Hindu epic, and the legend of Lord Ram travelled across the breadth of Asia and beyond. In this concluding chapter I want to consider and distil a few insights that become apparent in light of this study. The most puzzling facet of the Ramayana's transmission is why it occurred in the first place. There are certainly other epics, in Hinduism as well as other religions, that too are riveting in their detail and narrative. But none achieved the prominence and acceptability that the Ramayana did. More importantly, this cultural diffusion took place despite the full knowledge in populations that the Ramayana was a "foreign import" from India. Cultural constructions of identity, whether at the individual, social, or national level, typically favour stories of greatness that are native. The challenge was made more insurmountable by the fact that societies that were telling stories of the Ramayana were at times, religiously speaking, antithetical to its message. Then, why would these variegated societies want to tell and propagate the story of Lord Ram? Why does his figure inspire those that are not his own? The answer certainly doesn't lie in the inherent persuasiveness of Hinduism, as the transmission of the Ramayana in Asia probably owes more to Buddhism and its missionaries, than Hindus. Although, having said this, it probably does speak to a wider acceptability and universalism of Hindu ethics. Nonetheless, we don't have an explanation for the implausible transmission of the Ramayana to Thailand, Cambodia, Indonesia, Malaysia, Laos, Myanmar, Philippines, China and Tibet, Japan, Sri Lanka, Nepal, and in the Hindu Diaspora, as has been described in this book. An enquiry into this question is important to shed light on both, the cultural evolution of Asia as well as the singular genius of the Hindu epic and its many interlocutors.

One of the factors that has aided the fate of the Ramayana has been the simplicity and accompanying moral force of its narrative. The storyline is not overburdened by an unmanageable host of characters like the Mahabharata, but is equally convincing in its description of valour, courage, and moralism. This was a great strength in terms of its transmission via oral tradition, making it easier for people to remember and retell its story in the pre-modern era. More importantly however, the nature of moralism the Ramayana propagates seems to have an unrivalled force as well. The incredible sacrifice for family values, the dharma of a king, the evil of greed and hubris and its overcoming, the victory of righteousness etc. are all timeless messages that seemingly transcended the limits of space. The Ramayana in that sense represents the better angels of our nature and helps firmly ground the place of morality in society and the role of epics in informing them. The Ramayana offers a comprehensive moral code and there are an infinite number of characters that can be relied upon to impart lessons for members of society, for instance that of an ideal king in the image of Lord Ram, the ideal partnership in the image of Lord Ram and Sita, an ideal follower in the image of Hanuman, an ideal brother in the image of Lakshman etc. These moral lessons were crucial for a desirable social order to emerge in these societies, and was mobilised by people in different ranks to organise, impart, and perform ethical conduct. This is because the characters in the epic, especially Lord Rama, Sita, and Hanuman, served as moral exemplars, and their actions and choices provide valuable lessons on duty, righteousness, and the importance of dharma. The text delves into philosophical and spiritual aspects of life, exploring concepts such as the nature of reality, the purpose of human existence, and the path to spiritual enlightenment. It has therefore been a source of inspiration for philosophical discussions and reflections.

The second reason the Ramayana has travelled so well has been its ability to adapt to local conditions, thus enabling its diffusion across geographies. There has been a litany of studies on the phenomenon of cultural hybridity, in which artefacts of two distinct cultures interact, adapt, and merge to forge hybrid versions of themselves. Ultimately, culture is as fluid a phenomenon as any other and it is often difficult to delineate its ownership, boundaries, or even precise characteristics. On similar lines, due to the absence of gatekeepers, the Ramayana has been able to adapt to diverse cultural contexts by incorporating local myths, customs, and traditions. As it spread to different regions, local storytellers often infused their own cultural elements into the narrative, making it more relatable to the people living in those areas.

On the surface level, the Hindu epic has been translated into numerous languages over the centuries. As it reached different geographies, it was translated into local languages, making it accessible to a broader audience. This linguistic adaptation helped in the assimilation of the Hindu epic into diverse cultural settings. But at a deeper level, the Ramayana, while rooted in Hinduism, has also been adapted to suit the unique religious and cultural sensibilities of different regions. In some cases, it has coexisted with local belief systems and has been integrated into syncretic forms of worship. This adaptability has allowed the Ramayana to transcend its original religious boundaries. For instance, the Cambodian Ramayana shows monkeys in a relatively poorer light because of their status in Khmer culture. The Indonesian Ramayana, shows Sita as a fierce, bold, and assertive character, because of the gendered dynamics of its society. The Malaysian and Filipino Ramayana turns the religious antecedents of the Hindu epic on its head, offering instead an Islamic version. The Filipino Ramayana of course, famously replaces Lord Ram's monkey army with water buffalos and crocodiles. The Laotian and Sri Lankan Ramayanas are more sympathetic in their rendition of Ravan. The Chinese Ramayana and Japanese Ramayana are heavily influenced by Buddhist texts, but the Tibetan version, despite its prominence in the spread of Buddhism, does not. To answer A.K. Ramanujan's question on "how many Ramayanas?", there have been as many versions of the Ramayana as there are local cultures of worship for Lord Ram.

The third reason behind the extensive transmission of the Ramayana has been its nature and effect on political-power dynamics in the region. It has been documented that the

Indian Ocean Region was a hotbed of cultural globalisation. Despite this, with increase in cultural heterogeneity, there was no increase in conflict in this region. To some extent, the story of the Ramayana's transmission clarifies why this may have been the case. The Ramayana, and its geographical source, India, could capably act as a spiritual anchor as long as Indian kingdoms did not threaten the political might of these distant empires. Separated by a large ocean and the Himalayan ranges, India was close enough to offer spiritual guidance, but also sufficiently distant enough to not threaten local legitimacy of chieftains. This allowed political opportunists to mobilise, or at the very least permit the dissemination of, the Ramayana's message. Hinduism was neither an evangelical force, and nor were Indian kingdoms keen on such an Eastward expansion considering the rather bountiful regions they governed. In fact, following this logic, it is precisely in Sri Lanka and Nepal, two countries that are closest to the origins of the Ramayana that its message has encountered resistance. Bhanubhakta's Ramayana gained prominence in Nepal because it was the first rendering in Nepalese language, and challenged the dominance of Sanskrit versions. Similarly, the restoring of Ravan's character as a virtuous and in Sri Lanka is also a Sinhalese nationalist project that is seen in defiance of ostensible Indian cultural hegemony. In both these states, the Hindu epic, which is an export from India, becomes an instrument to challenge that very Indian cultural identity in distinction to a Nepali and Sri Lankan national identity. On the other hand, in other South East Asian geographies, such resistance was not encountered. In fact, respective monarchs and chieftains were pleased to integrate and use the Ramayana's moral force for the making of their social order(s). It is in the absence of hegemonic possibilities that the politics of cultural transmission is most effective. This suggests that the process of cultural transmission is more successful when it is bottom-up rather than top-down.

A strong example of the success of the transmission of the Ramayana in South East Asia was the celebration of the "Realising Rama" dance production organised by the Committee on Culture and Information of the Association of Southeast Asian Nations (ASEAN), a grouping of which India is not a member. It was officially labelled as the ASEAN Flagship Voyage, and was "conceived in March 1997 as a high-impact programme that would promote cultural awareness of ASEAN both within and outside the region". Performers from nine ASEAN countries, led by Thailand, were part of this exercise and were chosen on the basis of their mastery of their native traditional dances. The "Realising Rama" performance "had its world premiere at the Grand Theatre in Hanoi, Vietnam on 16 December 1998, during the Sixth ASEAN Summit Meeting. From September to October 1999, it was performed in the Philippines, Indonesia, Brunei Darussalam, Singapore and Malaysia. From March to April 2000, it toured Thailand, Lao PDR, Myanmar and Cambodia".[157] It helped build a cultural bridge to India:

> In North Asia, where the Ramayana is unknown, it was met with little curiosity or enthusiasm. In Europe, it was presented only for invited guests among the bureaucratic and diplomatic community. Realizing Rama was perhaps most well received in India, for not only were audiences accustomed to seeing variations of the Ramayana, the production played to India's cultural

> pride as the birthplace of the original text. Indian critics were uniformly enthusiastic, expressing no conflict of misrepresentation with the production's concision and stylistic fusion. That it was brought to India was perhaps seen by Indians as a form of respect, though Southeast Asian cultures had long before adapted the text to their own cultural specificities. Lindsay emphasizes the text's repositioning among the various audiences: "Realizing Rama's statement of otherness was also against 'Asia.' The choice of the Ramayana, and the way that choice was portrayed, stated that ASEAN is not India, but also, and more significantly, is not East Asia, where the Ramayana is not found" (2009).[158]

The "Realising Rama" theatrical project was commissioned in the aftermath of the 1997 economic crisis and was the first state-supported pan-ASEAN collaboration. The adaption of the Ramayana in South East Asia is so complete, that in an era of social turmoil, they turned to the epic to forge greater cohesion, both within and amongst their countries. Its transmission also came full circle, as it was the dramatic performance of the Ramayana that became a source of soft power for ASEAN countries in their dealings with India.

The inauguration of the Ram Mandir in Ayodhya is not merely significant for Hindus in India. It is a living monument for the cultural history of Asia and beyond. If there is a single lesson one can synthesise from the transmission of the Ramayana to these various countries, it is that the Ramayana and Lord Ram transcend the boundaries of religion. In that sense, the temple in Ayodhya is not a representation of the victory of any religious group over another. Such a view would be terribly short-sighted. Rather, the Ram Mandir is a celebration of a timeless and universal moralism and cultural ethos that has guided Indians of all stripes and other Asians, Hindus, Buddhists, and Muslims alike, for centuries. The Return of Lord Ram to Ayodhya, just as Rising India returns to the table of great powers, is befitting of her history, her aspirations, and her message to the peoples of the world. And, in our era of conflict and strife, is there a better message than that of dharma delivered by Lord Ram?

References

1. Francis Fukuyama, "The End of History?" The National Interest, no. 16 (1989): 3–18. http://www.jstor.org/stable/24027184.
2. Kishore Mahbubani, "Can Asians Think?" The National Interest, no. 52, 1998, pp. 27–35. JSTOR, http://www.jstor.org/stable/42897102.
3. Hamid Dabashi, Can Non-Europeans Think? London, England: Zed Books, 2021.
4. Paula Richman interview with Lalitha Venkat, "Paula Richman: Ramayana is a global text and global piece of theatre," December 14, 2008, Narthaki, https://www.narthaki.com/info/intervw/intrv109q.html.
5. Andrew Phillips and J.C. Sharman, International Order in Diversity: War, Trade and Rule in the Indian Ocean. Cambridge: Cambridge University Press, 2015.
6. Diana Eck, India: A Sacred Geography. 1st ed. New York: Harmony Books, 2012, p. 53
7. Amitav Acharya, "How Ideas Spread: Whose Norms Matter? Norm Localization and Institutional Change in Asian Regionalism". International Organization 58, no. 2 (2004): 239–75. http://www.jstor.org/stable/3877858.
8. Ravi Dutt Bajpai, "Ramayana: The Indian Epic and Its Relevance to Global IR," E-IR, https://www.e-ir.info/2023/08/17/ramayana-the-indian-epic-and-its-relevance-to-global-ir/.
9. Rabindranath Tagore, Nationalism. Macmillan, 1917.
10. "Swami Vivekananda and His 1893 Speech," https://www.artic.edu/swami-vivekananda-and-his-1893-speech.
11. T. Sasitharan, "Ramayana: A Cross-Cultural Phenomenon," https://www.esplanade.com/offstage/arts/ramayana-a-cross-cultural-phenomenon.
12. S.N. Desai. Hinduism in Thai Life. Popular Prakashan, 2005.

13. Outlook Web Desk, "Ram And The Many Ramayanas Outside India," Outlook Magazine, 23 October 2022, https://www.outlookindia.com/national/explained-the-many-ramayanas-outside-india-news-227482.
14. Frank E. Reynolds, Three Ramayana, Rama Jataka, and Ramakien: A Comparative Study of Hindu and Buddhist Traditions. University of California Press, 1991. https://publishing.cdlib.org/ucpressebooks/view?docId=ft3j49n8h7&chunk.id=d0e3418&toc.id=d0e3418&brand=eschol.
15. Sun Tawalwongsri, "The Creative Choreography for Nang Yai (Thai traditional shadow puppet theatre) Ramakien, Wat Ban Don, Rayong Province," Fine Arts International Journal, Srinakharinwirot University, no. 14-2 (2010). https://core.ac.uk/download/pdf/228515049.pdf.
16. Chollada Mongkol, A Comparative Study Of Dasakanthain Various Versions of The Ramakien. Graduate School Silpakorn University, 2017. http://202.44.135.157/dspace/bitstream/123456789/1195/1/56202205.pdf.
17. Reena Marwah, Reimagining India-Thailand Relations: A Multilateral and Bilateral Perspective. World Scientific, 2020.
18. S. Slngaravelu, "The Episode of Maiyarab in the Thai Ramakien and its Possible Relationship to Tamil Folklore," Journal of Siam Society (1984) 21-37. https://thesiamsociety.org/wp-content/uploads/1986/03/JSS_074_0d_Singaravelu_EpisodeOfMaiyarabInRamakianAndTamilFolklore.pdf.
19. A.K. Ramanujan, The Collected Essays of A. K. Ramanujan. Vinay Dharwadker (ed.), Oxford University Press, 1999. https://www.trans-techresearch.net/wp-content/uploads/2015/05/three-hundred-Ramayanas-A-K-Ramanujan.pdf.
20. Srisurang Poolthupya, "How the Ramakien Heritage survives in Thailand," The Journal of the Royal Institute of Thailand, vol. 1 (2009) p. 39. http://legacy.orst.go.th/royin2014/upload/246/FileUpload/2537_3200.pdf.
21. University of Michigan, "Thailand," Online Exhibits. https://apps.lib.umich.edu/online-exhibits/exhibits/show/the-career-of-rama/beyond-valmiki/thailand.
22. A.K. Ramanujan, The Collected Essays of A. K. Ramanujan. Vinay Dharwadker (ed.), Oxford University Press, 1999. https://www.trans-techresearch.net/wp-content/uploads/2015/05/three-hundred-Ramayanas-A-K-Ramanujan.pdf.

23. S. Slngaravelu, "The Rama Story in The Thai Cultural Tradition," Journal of Siam Society, 50-69. https://thesiamsociety.org/wp-content/uploads/1982/03/JSS_070_0g_Singaravelu_RamaStoryInThaiCulturalTradition.pdf.
24. Ibid.
25. Karmveer Singh."Cultural Dimensions of India–Thailand Relations: A Historical Perspective". History and Sociology of South Asia, no. 16(2), 77-92. https://doi.org/10.1177/22308075221098265
26. Ibid.
27. Srisurang Poolthupya, "King Rama VI's Promotion of Khon and Drama in General,"The Journal of the Royal Institute of Thailand, vol. II (2012). http://legacy.orst.go.th/royin2014/upload/246/FileUpload/2652_5035.pdf.
28. S.R. Praveen, "Ayutthaya: The other Ayodhya," The Hindu. 1 August 2019. https://www.thehindu.com/society/history-and-culture/the-deep-and-enduring-cultural-impact-of-the-ramayana-reverberates-in-thailand-from-its-national-epic-to-the-names-of-kings/article28771489.ece.
29. https://koreascience.kr/article/JAKO201135766043858.page.
30. Srisurang Poolthupya, "How the Ramakien Heritage survives in Thailand," The Journal of the Royal Institute of Thailand, vol. 1 (2009). http://legacy.orst.go.th/royin2014/upload/246/FileUpload/2537_3200.pdf.
31. Mya Gosling, The Ramayana in Contemporary Thailand. University of Michigan (2005). https://deepblue.lib.umich.edu/handle/2027.42/149097.
32. Karmveer Singh."Cultural Dimensions of India–Thailand Relations: A Historical Perspective". History and Sociology of South Asia, no. 16(2), 77-92. https://doi.org/10.1177/22308075221098265.
33. Saveros Pou, "Indigenization of Rāmāyaṇa in Cambodia." Asian Folklore Studies 51, no. 1 (1992): 89–102. https://doi.org/10.2307/1178423.
34. Siyonn Sophearith, "The Life of The Ramayana In Ancient Cambodia: A Study Of The Political, Religious And Ethical Roles Of An Epic Tale In Real Time," https://cdn.angkordatabase.asia/libs/docs/publications/the-life-of-the-ramayana-in-ancient-cambodia-a-study-of-the-political-religious-and-ethical-roles-of-an-epic-tale-in-real-time/Siyonn-Sophearith_UDAYA06-07-2006-r.pdf.

35. Trent Walker, "Epic: From Reamker," Manoa 34, no. 1 (2021): 11-14. https://doi.org/10.1353/man.2021.0018.
36. Judith M. Jacob, Reamker (Rāmakerti): The Cambodian Version of the Rāmāyaṇa, Psychology Press, (1986).
37. Saveros Pou, "Indigenization of Rāmāyaṇa in Cambodia." Asian Folklore Studies 51, no. 1 (1992): 89–102. https://doi.org/10.2307/1178423.
38. Saveros Pou, "Indigenization of Rāmāyaṇa in Cambodia." Asian Folklore Studies 51, no. 1 (1992): 89–102. https://doi.org/10.2307/1178423.
39. Judith M. Jacob, Reamker (Rāmakerti): The Cambodian Version of the Rāmāyaṇa, Psychology Press, (1986).
40. Siyonn Sophearith, "The Life of The Ramayana In Ancient Cambodia: A Study Of The Political, Religious And Ethical Roles Of An Epic Tale In Real Time," https://cdn.angkordatabase.asia/libs/docs/publications/the-life-of-the-ramayana-in-ancient-cambodia-a-study-of-the-political-religious-and-ethical-roles-of-an-epic-tale-in-real-time/Siyonn-Sophearith_UDAYA06-07-2006-r.pdf.
41. Mandakranta Bose, (ed.), The Ramayana Revisited (New York, 2004; Oxford Academic, 20 Apr. 2005), https://doi.org/10.1093/0195168321.001.0001.
42. Ibid.
43. Siyonn Sophearith, "The Life of The Ramayana In Ancient Cambodia: A Study Of The Political, Religious And Ethical Roles Of An Epic Tale In Real Time," https://cdn.angkordatabase.asia/libs/docs/publications/the-life-of-the-ramayana-in-ancient-cambodia-a-study-of-the-political-religious-and-ethical-roles-of-an-epic-tale-in-real-time/Siyonn-Sophearith_UDAYA06-07-2006-r.pdf.
44. Ibid.
45. The British Library, The Ramayana in Southeast Asia: (4) Indonesia and Malaysia,
https://blogs.bl.uk/asian-and-african/2014/05/the-ramayana-in-southeast-asia-4-indonesia-and-malaysia.html.
46. Malini Saran and Vinod C. Khanna, The Ramayana in Indonesia. Ravi Dayal, 2004.
47. Ibid.

48. Monidipa Dey, "The trail of Rama's tale: Ramayana's influence on India and Indonesia," Financial Express, 4 August 2020, https://www.financialexpress.com/lifestyle/the-trail-of-ramas-tale-ramayanas-influence-on-india-and-indonesia/2040834/.

49. Helen Creese, "Rāmāyaṇa Traditions in Bali," Brill, https://www.jstor.org/stable/10.1163/j.ctt1w76w8d.9.

50. Raghu Gururaj, "Sriwijaya-Nalanda Knowledge Trail," Transcontinental Times, 6 June 2021, https://www.transcontinentaltimes.com/author/raghu-gururaj/page/5/.

51. Malini Saran and Vinod C. Khanna, The Ramayana in Indonesia. Ravi Dayal, 2004.

52. Stuart Robson, "the Ramayana in Java and Bali: Chapters from its literary history," in Traces of the Ramayana and Mahabharata in Javanese and Malay Literature. Choo Ming Ding and Willem van der Molen (eds.), ISEAS Publishing, 2018. https://www.degruyter.com/document/doi/10.1355/9789814786584/html.

53. Dharma Negara Kumbhakarṇa in Kakawin Ramayana.

54. Malini Saran and Vinod C. Khanna, The Ramayana in Indonesia. Ravi Dayal, 2004.

55. Soewito Santoso, Ramayana Kakawin is the Old-Javanese or Indonesian Ramayana. New Delhi: International Academy of Indian Culture (1980). https://archive.org/details/RamayanaKakawinVol.3.

56. Tom Hunter, "The Ramayana in Indonesia by Malini Saran and Vinod C. Khanna," Asian Theatre Journal, Spring, 2005, Vol. 22, No. 1 (Spring, 2005), pp. 161-163.

57. M. Rajantherana, Krishanan Maniamb, Silllalee S. Kandasamyc, Samikkanu Jabamoney Ishak Samuel, International Journal of Innovation, Creativity and Change, no. 7(6) (2019). https://www.ijicc.net/images/vol7iss6/7624_Rajantheran_2019_E_R.pdf.

58. The British Library, The Ramayana in Southeast Asia: (4) Indonesia and Malaysia, https://blogs.bl.uk/asian-and-african/2014/05/the-ramayana-in-southeast-asia-4-indonesia-and-malaysia.html.

59. Richard O. Winstedt (ed.), A History of Classical Malay Literature. Kuala Lumpur: Oxford UP, 1972.

60. University of Michigan, "Malaysia", Online Exhibits. https://apps.lib.umich.edu/online-exhibits/exhibits/show/the-career-of-rama/beyond-valmiki/malaysia.

61. S. Singaravelu, "A Comparative Study of The Sanskrit, Tamil, Thai And Malay Versions of The Story of Rama With Special Reference To The Process of Acculturation In The Southeast Asian 'Versions'," https://thesiamsociety.org/wp-content/uploads/1968/03/JSS_056_2b_Singaravelu_SanskritTamilThaiAndMalayStoryOfRama.pdf
62. Shekhar Sen, "Review: Hikayat Seri Rama — The Malay Ramayana Harry Aveling," EducationWorld September 2021. https://www.educationworld.in/malaysian-ramayana/.
63. Arshia Sattar, "Rama of Adam's family: Arshia Sattar reviews 'Hikayat Seri Rama: The Malay Ramayana', Translated by Harry Aveling," The Hindu, 20 march 2021. https://www.thehindu.com/books/rama-of-adams-family-arshia-sattar-reviews-hikayat-seri-rama-the-malay-ramayana-translated-by-harry-aveling/article34105801.ece.
64. Shekhar Sen, "Review: Hikayat Seri Rama — The Malay Ramayana Harry Aveling," EducationWorld September 2021. https://www.educationworld.in/malaysian-ramayana/.
65. Ghulam-Sarwar Yousof, "Southeast Asian Adaptations of the Ramayana and their Use inthe Indonesian-Malaysian Shadow Play with Special Reference to Characterization," Malaysian Journal of Performing and Visual Arts, no. 1 (2015). https://ejournal.um.edu.my/index.php/MJPVA/article/view/2042/376.
66. Waradet Mesangrutdharakul, "The Tamil's Ramayana at Batu Cave, Malaysia. A Comparative Case Study of Thai Ramayana and Valmiki's Ramayana," Review of Integrated Business and Economics, no. 5 (2016). http://sibresearch.org/uploads/3/4/0/9/34097180/riber_s16-218_100-106.pdf.
67. Arshia Sattar, "Rama of Adam's family: Arshia Sattar reviews 'Hikayat Seri Rama: The Malay Ramayana', Translated by Harry Aveling," The Hindu, 20 march 2021. https://www.thehindu.com/books/rama-of-adams-family-arshia-sattar-reviews-hikayat-seri-rama-the-malay-ramayana-translated-by-harry-aveling/article34105801.ece
68. The British Library, The Ramayana in Southeast Asia: (2) Thailand and Laos, 28 April 2014. https://blogs.bl.uk/asian-and-african/2014/04/the-ramayana-in-southeast-asia-2-thailand-and-laos.html.
69. Official Website, Phra Lak Phra Lam. http://phralakphralam.com/phralak_phralam_en/le-phralak-phralam/les-personnages/.

70. Smai Wannaudorn, and Pathom Hongsuwan. Phra Lak Phra Lam: The Representation of Cultural Ecology in Lao Society," The Journal of Lao Studies, no. 5(1) (2014): 94-107. https://www.laostudies.org/system/files/subscription/JLS-v5-i1-Aug2014-Wannaudorn-Hongsuwan.pdf.
71. Patit Paban Mishra, "Cultural Contribution Of India To South-East Asia : A Case Study Of Laos." Proceedings of the Indian History Congress 56 (1995): 870–76. http://www.jstor.org/stable/44158748.
72. Manasi Dhanorkar, "Phralak Phralam – Ramleela, Lao style!" https://penangdiaries.wordpress.com/2017/10/25/phralak-phralam-mount-phu-si-garavek-the-lao-connection-to-ramayan/.
73. Rakasmani, Kusuma, "The Story of Rama in Lao Folktale", in Ramayana Its Universal Appeal and Global Role, L.P. Vyas (ed.) Delhi,1992, p. 72.
74. SEACOM South East Asia Communication Centre, "Thai and Lao traditions of the Ramayana," 17 May 2024. https://seacomberlin.wordpress.com/2014/05/17/thai-and-lao-traditions-of-the-ramayana/.
75. Image of "Phralak-Phralam," Digital Conservation Facility, Laos Southeast Asia Digital Library. https://sea.lib.niu.edu/islandora/object/SEAImages%3A1543.
76. Official Website, Phra Lak Phra Lam. http://phralakphralam.com/phralak_phralam_en/le-phralak-phralam/les-personnages/.
77. Parul Pandya Dhar (ed.) The Multivalence of an Epic Retelling the Rāmāyaṇa in South India and Southeast Asia. Routledge, 2023.
78 Ibid.
79. British Library, The Ramayana in Southeast Asia: (2) Thailand and Laos, 28 April 2014. https://blogs.bl.uk/asian-and-african/2014/04/the-ramayana-in-southeast-asia-2-thailand-and-laos.html.
80. Gisa Jähnichen, "Re-Designing the Role of Phalak and Phalam in Modern Lao Ramayana," Journal of Arts Discourse, no. 6 (2010): 1-42.
81. British Library, The Ramayana in Southeast Asia: (3) Burma, 05 May 2014.https://blogs.bl.uk/asian-and-african/2014/05/the-ramayana-in-southeast-asia-3-burma.html.

82. U.T. Kaung, "The Ramayana Drama in Myanmar," Journal of the Siam Society, no. 90(1-2) (2002): 137-148. https://www.uclmyanmar.org/wp-content/uploads/2016/01/8-The-Ramayana-Drama-in-Myanmar.pdf.
83. Ibid.
84. Library of Congress, "Ramayana," 1870https://www.loc.gov/item/2021668039/.
85. Pe Maung Tin, U.,"Cultural Activities in Konbaung Period. Pt. one. The Story of How the Ramayana Came to Burma", The Working People's Daily, Sunday Supplement (14 Mar. 1965).
86. https://blogs.bl.uk/asian-and-african/2014/05/the-ramayana-in-southeast-asia-3-burma.html.
87. U.T. Kaung, "The Ramayana Drama in Myanmar," Journal of the Siam Society, no. 90(1-2) (2002): 137-148. https://www.uclmyanmar.org/wp-content/uploads/2016/01/8-The-Ramayana-Drama-in-Myanmar.pdf.
88. U Paw Hnyun, "Scenes from the Thiri Rama, the Burmese adaptation of the Ramayana," The MET, ca. 1870–85. https://www.metmuseum.org/art/collection/search/848697.
89. Michael Symes. An account of an embassy to the kingdom of Ava sent by the Governor-General of India, in the year 1795.W. Bulmer and Co., and sold by G. and W. Nicol and by J. Wright, (1800): 177-178.
90. Kenneth Robert and Henderson Mackenzie, "Burmah and the Burmese," Journal of the Asiatic Soc. of Bengal, no. 8, p. 535.
91. George Scott, Sir. The Burman, His Life and Notions, by Shway Yoe. 3rd ed. 1910. p.295.
92. U.T. Kaung, "The Ramayana Drama in Myanmar," Journal of the Siam Society, no. 90(1-2) (2002): 137-148. https://www.uclmyanmar.org/wp-content/uploads/2016/01/8-The-Ramayana-Drama-in-Myanmar.pdf.
93. Official Website. Embassy of India, Manila, Philippines. https://www.eoimanila.gov.in/eoi.php?id=bilateral-cultural-relations/.
94. Juan R. Francisco, The Maharadia Lawana. Philippine Folklore Society, 1969.
95. Jordan Clark, "Maharadia Lawana, the Maranao Epic," 27 July 2021. https://www.aswangproject.com/maharadia-lawana-epic/.
96. Ibid.

97. Juan R. Francisco, Notes on Islamic Literature in the Philippines, University of Michigan (2007), pp. 43-44.
98. Juan R. Francisco, The Maharadia Lawana. Philippine Folklore Society, 1969, pp. 195.
99. ASEAN-India Centre at RIS, Act East: ASEAN-India Shared Cultural Heritage, RIS, 2019. https://aseanindiacentre.org.in/sites/default/files/Publication/ASEAN%20–%20India%20Shared%20Cultural%20Heritage_SECURE-web_0.pdf.
100. YuLongyuandMengZhaoyi,HistoryofOrientalLiterature.Beijing, 2001. https://archive.org/details/dongfangwenxuesh0000unse/page/n3/mode/2up.
101. Devdutt Pattnaik, "Tibetan Ramayana," 12 March2023, Mid-Day, https://www.mid-day.com/news/opinion/article/tibetan-ramayana-23274778.
102. Xianlin, J. (2012). The Ramayana in China. China Report, 48(1-2), 187-198. https://doi.org/10.1177/000944551104800210.
103. Santosh N. Desai. "Ramayana--An Instrument of Historical Contact and Cultural Transmission between India and Asia." The Journal of Asian Studies 30, no. 1 (1970): 5–20. https://doi.org/10.2307/2942721.
104. K. Watanabe, "The Oldest Record of The Ramayana Ina Chinese Buddhist Writing," 99-103. https://core.ac.uk/reader/212151540.
105. B.R. Deepak, "How Lord Ram reached China," The Sunday Guardian, 8 August 2020. https://sundayguardianlive.com/opinion/lord-ram-reached-china.
106. B.R. Deepak, "Hanuman and Sun Wukong: How Indian and Chinese literary images integrate," The Sunday Guardian, 27December 2020.https://sundayguardianlive.com/news/hanuman-sun-wukong-indian-chinese-literary-images-integrate.
107. Yuyun Xue, "Study on the Time and Route of the Introduction of Ramayana into the Dai Ethnic Area of China," Advances in Social Science, Education and Humanities Research, no. 588, proceedings of the 2nd International Conference on Language, Communication and Culture Studies (ICLCCS 2021).https://www.google.com/url?sa=t&rct=j&q=&esrc=s&source=web&cd=&ved=2ahUKEwjFnoSWtq-DAxV6cGwGHQehDFQQFnoECBIQAQ&url=https%3A%2F%2Fwww.atlantis-press.com%2Farticle%2F125962046.pdf&usg=AOvVaw2mYVsn9L7hjQgN4Y8Gal0M&opi=89978449.

108. Chitra Unnithan, "To learn Hindi, Chinese turn to Ramayana," The Times of India, 26 October 2012. https://timesofindia.indiatimes.com/city/ahmedabad/to-learn-hindi-chinese-turn-to-ramayana/articleshow/16961092.cms.
109 . Ulrike Roesler, "The adventures of Rāma, Sītā and Rāvaṇa in Tibet," in The Other Ramayana Women, John Brockington, Mandakranta Bose, Mary Brockington (eds.), Routledge, 2016. https://www.taylorfrancis.com/chapters/edit/10.4324/9781315678252-5/adventures-rāma-sītā-rāvaṇa-tibet-ulrike-roesler.
110 Jong, J. W. de. "An Old Tibetan Version of the Ramāyāṇa." T'oung Pao 58, no. 1/5 (1972): 190–202. http://www.jstor.org/stable/4527910.
111. The Dunhuang version was introduced and analysed in some detail by F.W. Thomas (1929) on the basis of the manuscripts A to D; J.K. Balbir used manuscript E, edited the text and translated it into French in 1963 under the title L'Histoire de Rāma en tibétain d'après des manuscrits de Touenhouang. De Jong was the first to edit and translate the text in full on the basis of all available material and studied it in considerable detail. His articles are compiled in de Jong 1994.
112. Ulrike Roesler, "The adventures of Rāma, Sītā and Rāvaṇa in Tibet," in The Other Ramayana Women, John Brockington, Mandakranta Bose, Mary Brockington (eds.), Routledge, 2016. https://www.taylorfrancis.com/chapters/edit/10.4324/9781315678252-5/adventures-rāma-sītā-rāvaṇa-tibet-ulrike-roesler.
113. Devdutt Pattnaik, "Tibetan Ramayana," 12 March2023, Mid-Day, https://www.mid-day.com/news/opinion/article/tibetan-ramayana-23274778.
114. Ulrike Roesler, "The adventures of Rāma, Sītā and Rāvaṇa in Tibet," in The Other Ramayana Women, John Brockington, Mandakranta Bose, Mary Brockington (eds.), Routledge, 2016. https://www.taylorfrancis.com/chapters/edit/10.4324/9781315678252-5/adventures-rāma-sītā-rāvaṇa-tibet-ulrike-roesler.
115. Abiral Kumar, "Implications of Ramayana in Indo-Tibetan Interactions:A Study," Tibet Policy Journal, no. 2 (2018): 42-53. https://tibetpolicy.net/wp-content/uploads/2019/11/TPI-2018-Eng.pdf.
116. Nancy Lin, "Döndrup Gyel and the Remaking of the Tibetan Ramayana," in Modern Tibetan Literature and Social Change,

Lauran R. Hartley and Patricia Schiaffini-Vedani (eds.), New York, USA: Duke University Press, 2008. https://www.degruyter.com/document/doi/10.1515/9780822381433-007/html.

117. Simran Sood, "A Tibetan Retelling of the Ramayana," 12 May 2023. https://enrouteindianhistory.com/a-tibetan-retelling-of-the-ramayana/#:~:text=Discovery%20of%20manuscripts%20in%20Dunhuang%20Caves%20in%201908.&text=There%20is%20no%20influence%20of,story%20is%20recounted%20in%20prose.

118 . Ulrike Roesler, "The adventures of Rāma, Sītā and Rāvaṇa in Tibet," in The Other Ramayana Women, John Brockington, Mandakranta Bose, Mary Brockington (eds.), Routledge, 2016. https://www.taylorfrancis.com/chapters/edit/10.4324/9781315678252-5/adventures-rāma-sītā-rāvaṇa-tibet-ulrike-roesler.

119. Akira Kiuchi, "Ramayana In Northern East Asia Tradition and Its Influences to Their Culture," International Conference of Hindu Studies, no. 1 (2023): https://conference.uhnsugriwa.ac.id/index.php/icohis/article/view/10.

120. Gaurav Sharma, "Ramayana(s) retold in Asia," The Hindu, 19 February 2012. https://www.thehindu.com/features/friday-review/theatre/ramayanas-retold-in-asia/article2909774.ece

121. Fabio Rambelli, "The Idea of India (Tenjiku) in Pre-Modern Japan: Issues of Signification and Representation in the Buddhist Translation of Cultures," in Buddhism Across Asia, Tansen Sen (ed.) volume 1, Singapore: ISEAS Publishing, 2014. https://doi.org/10.1355/9789814519335.

122. Robert P. Goldman and Sally J. Sutherland Goldman, "Ramayana," https://lakshminarayanlenasia.com/articles/Mittal_Thursby_The_Hindu_World.pdf#page=88.

123. https://www.google.co.in/books/edition/The_Ramayana_Tradition_In_Asia/uo1DPgAACAAJ?hl=en.

124. Madoka Fukuoka, Ramayana Theatre in Contemporary Southeast Asia, Routledge, 2023.

125. Godakumbura, C. E. "A Note on the Jānakīharaṇa." The Journal of the Ceylon Branch of the Royal Asiatic Society of Great Britain & Ireland 11 (1967): 93–98. http://www.jstor.org/stable/43483840.

126. Chittenjoor Kunhan Raja, Survey of Sanskrit. Bharatiya Vidya Bhavan, 1962. https://www.google.co.in/books/edition/Survey_of_Sanskrit_Literature/hutjAAAAMAAJ?hl=en.

127. Theodor Aufrecht, Ujjvalàdatta's commentary on the Uṇādisūtras, Bonn, Adolph Marcus, 1859, pp. xviii-xi.

128. Godakumbura, C. E. "A Note on the Jānakīharaṇa." The Journal of the Ceylon Branch of the Royal Asiatic Society of Great Britain & Ireland 11 (1967): 93–98. http://www.jstor.org/stable/43483840.

129. Goonatilake, Susantha. "Introduction to the Issue on the Rāmāyaṇa." Journal of the Royal Asiatic Society of Sri Lanka 59, no. 2 (2014): 1–21. http://www.jstor.org/stable/44809402.

130. See Heinz Bechert, "The Beginnings of Buddhist Historiography: Mahavamsa and Political Thinking", in Bardwell Smith (ed.), Religion and Legitimation of Power in Sri Lanka (Chambersburg, PA: Anima Books, 1978), pp. 1–12.

131. Richard Gombrich, 'The Vessantara Jataka, the Ramayana, and the Dasharatha Jataka', in Journal of the American Oriental Society, Vol. 105, no. 3 (1985), pp. 427–37.

132. Steven Collins, 'What is Literature in Pali?', in Sheldon Pollock (ed.), Literary Cultures in History: Reconstructions from South Asia (Berkeley: University of California Press, 2003), pp. 649–88.

133. Justin W. Henry & Sree Padma (2019) Lankapura: The Legacy of the Ramayana in Sri Lanka, South Asia: Journal of South Asian Studies, 42:4, 726-731, DOI: 10.1080/00856401.2019.1626127.

134. Henry, Justin W. "Explorations in the Transmission of the Ramayana in Sri Lanka." South Asia: Journal of South Asian Studies 42 (2019): 732 - 746.

135. Justin W. Henry & Sree Padma (2019) Lankapura: The Legacy of the Ramayana in Sri Lanka, South Asia: Journal of South Asian Studies, 42:4, 726-731, DOI: 10.1080/00856401.2019.1626127.

136. Henry, Justin W. "Explorations in the Transmission of the Ramayana in Sri Lanka." South Asia: Journal of South Asian Studies 42 (2019): 732 - 746.

137. Jonathan Walters, 'Vibhisana and Vijayanagar: An Essay on Geopolitics in Medieval Sri Lanka', in The Sri Lanka Journal of the Humanities, Vols. 17 and 18, nos. 1 and 2 (1991/1992), pp. 129–42.

138. Sree Padma (2019) Borders Crossed: Vibhishana in the Ramayana and Beyond, South Asia: Journal of South Asian Studies, 42:4, 747-767, DOI: 10.1080/00856401.2019.1631738.

139. "Bhanubhakta Ramayana inspires to learn sense of respect-Vice President," NepalNews.com, 5 October 2023. https://nepalnews.

com/s/nation/bhanubhakta-ramayana-inspires-to-learn-sense-of-respect-vice-president.

140. "Lord Ram was Nepali, India set up a 'fake Ayodhya', claims Nepal PM KP Oli," India Today, 14 July 2020. https://www.indiatoday.in/india/story/lord-ram-was-nepali-india-set-up-a-fake-ayodhya-claims-nepal-pm-kp-oli-1700220-2020-07-13.

141. Amish Raj Mulmi, "Nepal's Ramayanas," The Himalayan Magazine, 10 August 2020. https://www.himalmag.com/nepals-ramayanas-2020/.

142. Ibid.

143. Dhruba H. Adhikary, "A Nepali Ramayana For English Readers," The Rising Nepal, 8 July 2022. https://risingnepaldaily.com/news/13638.

144. Pratyoush Onta, "The Career of Bhanubhakta as a History of Nepali National Culture, 1940-1999, Studies in Nepal History and Society, no. 4(1) (1999): 65-136.

145. Amish Raj Mulmi, "Nepal's Ramayanas," The Himalayan Magazine, 10 August 2020. https://www.himalmag.com/nepals-ramayanas-2020/.

146. Ibid.

147. Richard Burghart, "The Disappearance and Reappearance of Janakpur." Kailash, https://himalaya.socanth.cam.ac.uk/collections/journals/kailash/pdf/kailash_06_04_03.pdf.

148. Pratyoush Onta, "Creating a Brave Nepali Nation in British India: The Rhetoric of Jāti Improvement, Rediscovery of Bhanubhakta and the Writing of BīrHistory", https://www.martinchautari.org.np/storage/files/sinhas-vol1-no1-pratyoush-onta.pdf.

149. Pratyoush Onta, "The Career of Bhanubhakta as a History of Nepali National Culture, 1940-1999, Studies in Nepal History and Society, no. 4(1) (1999): 65-136.

150. Rajesh Rai sasrr@nus.edu.sg & Chitra Sankaran (2011) Religion and the South Asian diaspora, South Asian Diaspora, 3:1, 5-13, DOI: 10.1080/19438192.2010.539030.

151. Derek Walcott, "Nobel Acceptance Speech: Fragments of an Epic Memory." 1992,

152. Richman, Paula. "A Diaspora Ramayana in Southall, Greater London." Journal of the American Academy of Religion 67, no. 1 (1999): 33–57. http://www.jstor.org/stable/1466032.

153. Afroz Taj and John Caldwell, "Lord Ram Plays the Parking Lot: Ramlila in the Diaspora," Asian Theatre Journal, Volume 37, Number 1, Spring 2020, pp. 200-227. https://muse.jhu.edu/article/757853/pdf.
154. Kumar Mahabir and Susan Chand, "The Phenomenon of Ramleela/ Ramlila Theatre in Trinidad," in Global Hindu Diaspora: Historical and Contemporary Perspectives, Kalpana Hiralal (ed.), Routledge 2017).
155. Milla C. Riggio, Performing in the Lap and at the Feet of God: Ramleela in Trinidad, 2006–2008, TDR / The Drama Review 54(1):106-149 (2010).
156. Sherry Ann Singh, The Ramayana Tradition and Socio-Religious Change in Trinidad 1917–1990, Ian Randle Publishers, 2012.
157. Nicanor G. Tiongson, "Realising Rama, Realising ASEAN," SPAFA Journal Vol. 10 No. 2. https://www.google.com/url?sa=t&rct=j&q=&esrc=s&source=web&cd=&ved=2ahUKEwiPnuCiw9WDAxV5TWwGHSuWAFsQFnoECA0QAQ&url=https%3A%2F%2Fwww.spafajournal.org%2Findex.php%2Fspafa1991journal%2Farticle%2Fview%2F320%2F312&usg=AOvVaw2jsL39sAFrBLXVoNFmFs4-&opi=89978449.
158. Catherine Diamond, The Impossibility of Performing "Asia," in Asia through Art and Anthropology: Cultural Translation Across Borders, Fuyubi Nakamura, Morgan Perkins, Olivier Krischer (eds.), Routledge, 2013.